When
Bamboo Bloom

When Bamboo Bloom

An Anthropologist in Taliban's Afghanistan

Patricia A. Omidian

WAVELAND

PRESS, INC.

Long Grove, Illinois

For information about this book, contact:
Waveland Press, Inc.
4180 IL Route 83, Suite 101
Long Grove, IL 60047-9580
(847) 634-0081
info@waveland.com
www.waveland.com

Map credits:
Map of Afghanistan, p. xii—Based on UN Map No. 3958 Rev. 6, July 2009. (Spelling of some names has been changed to reflect the spelling in the book.)
Ethnicity map, p. 5—Adapted by permission of the publisher from "The Taliban's Winning Strategy in Afghanistan" by Gilles Dorronsoro (Washington, DC: Carnegie Endowment for International Peace, 2009), p. 15. www.carnegieendowment.org
Drought map, p. 41—Adapted from United Nations World Food Programme (WFP) July 17, 2000.

For Jyan, Elizabeth, and Kian

For the people of Afghanistan:
May you always hold hope in front of you
And may peace come in your hearts and to your country

Contents

Acknowledgments

$\mathcal{E}$ven though I now live in Pakistan, I monitor the news of Afghanistan each day. Every bomb blast in Kabul brings a spate of messages between my friends and me, just to assure myself that everyone is OK. And, each time fighting breaks out in Karachi, more messages pass between us. Social networking sites and text messaging make life much easier: no one has to wait for news. The war in Afghanistan is not over, and with each bomb blast or targeted killing, hope, the backbone of Afghan resiliency, ebbs and then rises again in the lull before the next blast comes.

Ethnographies are never the work of one person in isolation. This book is no different. I never traveled alone in Afghanistan, and I rarely lived alone. I want to thank Sayed M. Yousef Mirbacha and his wife Gulcheen. They accepted me as a member of their family; we took care of each other for over seven years. They took the risk to take in a foreigner. I am an auntie to all their children. Without their great care and patient teaching of their language and culture, I would not have been able to do the kind of work I did. We were a multilingual family: I spoke Dari, a Persian dialect, with the parents; I spoke English with the children; and the family spoke Pashtu to each other. Because we lived in Pakistan for much of the time, the children also spoke Urdu. Together we moved to Kabul in 2002. Today, when I talk to any of the children, I hear their mother in the background telling me to come back to Kabul.

Mr. Aziz Yaqubi and Engineer Muslim were important traveling companions and stayed in touch after these excursions. Aziz is the best translator I have met, and his knowledge of computers and finance is amazing. He and I continued to work together on various projects for the American Friends Service Committee. He and his wonderful wife always made sure I felt welcome, comfortable, and safe. I would not be surprised if we find more chances to travel or work together in the future. Engineer Muslim returned to the army and to a position of command when things changed in 2001. I never could reconcile my image of him as a friendly family man with his stern demeanor as an army officer. He is a man of integrity and honesty. This book is also, in many ways, about and for these two brave men.

After I left Afghanistan in 2007, it took me a couple of years before I felt ready to write about my experiences. I started this book in 2009, telling friends and colleagues that all I had to do was write one page per day and at the end of a year I would have a book. It took the encouragement of Muna Bilgrami, Nafisa Rizvi, Amarah Makhdumi, and Haifah Alsaidi to get me started. We had formed a writers' group where they heard a number of my stories. My first draft was a disaster. I want to thank Nafisa for not giving up on me and encouraging me to continue. She accepted the next draft and gave incredible and detailed comments that improved it immensely.

Dr. Marcia A. Grant and Shireen Azfar, along with Zakir Thaver and Michael DeSouza, colleagues of mine at the time, also gave me an incredible amount of support, let me try out ideas, and put up with my moodiness when the writing hit a difficult place.

I thank Dr. H. R. Ahmad and his wife, Rafia, for their marvelous support and encouragement as I completed this book from our place in Karachi. I took a seven-month hiatus to complete the work. I kept my home (an apartment above theirs in Karachi). Without them I don't know how I could have finished this book, as they helped me in many ways—including letting me pay my rent late. I have to thank Mr. Inderyas Samuel, who took great care of my home, and continues to help me out, giving me time to work.

Without Nina Joy Lawrence, my partner in the development of the community Focusing model, the work with CHA would not have happened. She introduced me to Focusing and made sure I was able to get the training I needed. We meet on the Internet almost daily now to continue the intellectual development of our work and to spend time Focusing. Nina Joy, and her husband Dr. Robert Lawrence, shared the Fulbright residence in Peshawar in 1997–1998. We became close friends. They returned to Pakistan in 2000, giving Nina Joy and me the opportunity to work together. Over subsequent years, we have visited regularly. They made sure I had what I needed to write—friendship, long Internet conversations, and even longer conversations at their dining table in Corvallis. Bob checked his archive of photos to find one of me, in my shalwar kamees, to include in this book.

My son, Jyan Omidian, has had to put up with a mother who traveled a great deal, and he found one of the easiest ways to know what she was up to was to visit her. He came to Pakistan twice and Afghanistan once. In fact, he was in Afghanistan with me when George W. Bush initiated the war effort in Iraq. Thank you, Jyan, for your support, your caring, and your enthusiasm. I know you are getting tired of my stories, but you always let me know you are proud of me.

I also have to thank my brother, Lawrence Burton, for reading every chapter and making comments on what worked and what didn't. Larry wanted to know more about me and wanted to hear how my work changed me. He helped shape this work.

I want to thank Tom Curtin, my editor at Waveland, for his marvelous encouragement. Thanks also to Jeni Ogilvie, a patient copy editor, for her gentle editing of the work. We sent a lot of e-mails and had to deal with a significant time difference, but both Tom and Jeni were tolerant of changes I wanted to make. They both gave detailed advice. I thank them both for their wholehearted enthusiasm for this project.

Finally I must thank the Afghans with whom I lived and worked. Abdul Salam Rahimy, Salma Waqfi, Khala Mariam, Fariba Nawa, Naeem Azizian, and the late Mohammad Ali Tarshi (and his family). The list is endless. I learned in my travels how to stay hopeful and to look for kindness in small acts—where the gift to a guest might only be a cool cup of water. I owe a debt of gratitude to the many women, men, and children I met during my journeys. For all the horrors of war, drought, and uncertainty, the Afghans remained hospitable, kind, and patient with me. I learned that one could always laugh, even through tears. And that bamboo will bloom.

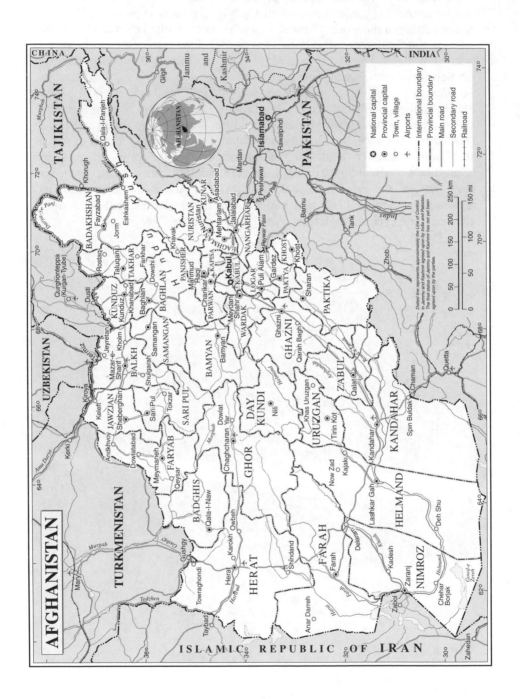

Introduction

$\mathcal{I}$ arrived in Pakistan in August 1997, after a long flight from the United States. It was to be a short-term adventure and I had only the barest of notions of what I would experience. I came because I thought it would help my career as an anthropologist; because I really wanted to live abroad; and because I had just gone through a divorce and wanted to make a new start in life. I had first visited Pakistan in 1988 and found it to be a place of contrasts: women wore colorful and varied clothing, while men all wore the same monochrome outfits; the streets were noisy with crowds of people and motor rickshaws, while behind the high walls of housing compounds people rarely spoke in loud voices. Most important for me, as a single woman and an outsider, the people were always hospitable. It was the kind of place an anthropologist should study. I had wanted to conduct my dissertation research there but the first Gulf War (August 1990 to March 1991) prevented that. At that time I also had a teenage son to raise, so I needed to wait to do any research abroad until after he had graduated from high school. That is what I did. Shortly after he moved to his college, I found myself on a Fulbright scholarship in Pakistan.

This was not the first time I had lived abroad. I had married an Iranian in Iran back in the 1970s, at a time when Iran was still a friend of the United States. I had the wonderful opportunity to live briefly there, when I took a short break from working toward my BA in Cultural Anthropology. My intention was to return there to do fieldwork at the graduate level, but that was not to be. Iran had a revolution. No problem, thought I: I can do my ethnographic fieldwork in Afghanistan, instead. That was not to be, either. Shortly after the Iranian revolution, the Soviet Union toppled the government in Afghanistan, placed its own person in power, and in 1979 the war between the Soviet-backed Afghan government and Afghan *mujahadeen* began in earnest and lasted ten years.

My interest in Afghanistan grew out of the contact I had with the Afghan refugee community in the United States, and in particular because of a certain

1

refugee family. My husband had a good friend from his high school days in Iran, and although this friend is Afghan, he spent much of his childhood in Iran. We helped sponsor him and his family, bringing them to the United States in the mid-1980s. It was through them that my interest in Afghanistan and the needs of refugees grew (Omidian 1996). It was also because of the issues I watched this family face that I started to become interested in the fields of mental health and the anthropology of emotions. Over the years I acquired a deepening interest in human resiliency and cultural factors that affect *psychosocial wellness*. That is, I am interested in the interrelationship of physical health, mental health, and life satisfaction for people who have experienced war, displacement, and resettlement, and how they have adapted to their situation. In the process of my research, I have collected information in Pashto (the language spoken by Pashtun people in Afghanistan and northwestern Pakistan) and Dari (the dialect of Persian spoken in Afghanistan) on labels for and categories of emotions, as they vary by age and gender. Most of my research on psychosocial wellness has been conducted on my own time, as my primary work involves being hired as a consulting applied anthropologist.

Anthropology and Aid Work

As an applied anthropologist I was often hired by an agency, either a governmental organization or a nongovernmental organization (NGO), to study an issue that was important to it. Although I rarely selected my research topic, or the parameters of the study, I was able to choose how to implement the process. It is the anthropological lens—the ability to view a culture holistically, to understand that any change in one area of a society will affect other areas, and to think comparatively—that makes our work valuable in disaster-response and development work. I found that there is an enormous need in development and aid work for anthropological skills, including qualitative research, ethnographic description, comparative approaches, and, maybe most important of all, the ability to write reports that are readable and easily applicable.

The descriptions in the following chapters highlight the kinds of issues I faced. Because I have a strong background in what is called "training of trainers," most of my work included some level of training and mentoring local staff, teaching them to conduct their own surveys, evaluations, or training (samples of two surveys appear in appendix A). Except for the psychosocial wellness research I was able to carry out in Herat, each project I was hired to do was unique: to conduct training, to carry out a survey, or to facilitate a process—such as strategic planning. Generally I would be asked what I could accomplish for a given amount of money, with full consideration of the goals of the project and for the locations designated by the hiring agency. I had to negotiate the best deal for myself that would ensure a successful result in the least amount of time, and with the least amount of travel. The cost of insurance to cover expatriates (expats for short) working in Afghanistan was high; therefore, the less travel inside the country the better. Afghanistan was, after all, a war zone. The agency funding the project, sometimes a donor agency rather than an NGO, was generally unwilling to pay for write-up time but would pay for time to do data analysis. I quickly discovered that for every two weeks in the field I needed approximately one week for analysis and write-up, and figured out a way to get paid for that. Whenever possible I also used analysis and write-up time as part of the training process for local staff.

One objective of each project was to train local staff to continue the work once I was gone. I tried to teach basic survey methods, methods that gave results but would not require a lot of money or technical expertise. In the Taliban's Afghanistan, where rural areas had no electricity, and hospitals and development agencies had only a limited use of generators, it was important to design projects that were not dependent on computer technology. In urban areas, where access to electricity and other services was greater, computer work was possible. Over time, it was heartening to see some of my training showing up in other places and on topics I had not covered.

In the following chapters, I have used a narrative approach to describe what it was like for me to conduct research, training, and program development in Afghanistan under the Taliban, while giving readers a sense of what it was like for the Afghans with whom I worked. I traveled in areas controlled by the Taliban and was subject to their laws. One of the restrictions I took seriously was the rule against taking photographs. The Taliban did not allow any pictures of people, and they often destroyed family albums found in the homes they searched. Although I have photos of my trips, I was very careful in how I took pictures and what I did with the digital camera's memory card. Had the Taliban stopped my colleagues and I and found a camera with pictures of people, we could have been in a great deal of trouble. As I looked for pictures to include in this book, I was surprised at how few I have from that time period. Many of the pictures of Kabul are from 2002, the year immediately after U.S. and NATO forces chased the Taliban from that city.

As a foreign woman traveling inside, I was not expected to wear the *chadari*—the all encompassing fabric worn over normal clothing that hides the woman from public view while she sees the world through a mesh of embroidered fabric that cuts off all peripheral vision. I was, however, expected to cover my body and hair, but in ways that varied from one location to the next and over time. In rural areas I tended to wear a large cotton shawl that was draped to cover most of my body but left my face open. In urban areas it was easier to wear the *hijab* (a floor length cotton coat and head scarf that was pinned in place).

To understand the research and training work that was carried out once my colleagues and I arrived in an area of Afghanistan, it is important to understand how I reached each location. Each trip inside took a great deal of time and effort for two reasons. First, logistics mattered. This was a war zone; my colleagues and I were at risk each time we went inside. I traveled with groups who opposed the Taliban—some openly defied them and their laws. Second, it was important to understand that the very act of travel could affect the study to be carried out, and in many ways travel was a study in and of itself. The problems and issues of logistics of travel were usually left out of the reports I wrote for the various agencies that hired me. Yet, they provide an important part of the record of the life of those with whom I worked or of the communities I studied.

As I share stories of the people met and the places visited, I want to describe Afghanistan as I saw it. Doing anthropology is an active process that involves hours and days of observation, sudden bursts of activity, and frequent demands of cultural sensitivity. At times, we must make decisions that have repercussions beyond one's self, and we often face dilemmas that have no easy answer. Yet, I, as an outsider, was not the only person making decisions that went against culture or safety. But safety was relative. Oppressive regimes force their citizens to go against their own cultural values, causing distress or worse. In Afghanistan, hospitality and the willingness to help others (important cultural practices) were sometimes set aside, though not willingly. Many times, families had to forfeit their right to decide their own rules, such as whether or not their children attended school or their daughters or wives could work. They had to refuse hospitality to friends or colleagues, or even refuse to help someone in need. On my trips to Afghanistan, I felt I had to make decisions that went against my core values. Yet, many of these decisions were actually not mine to make but were made on my behalf. Some of those caused problems, for myself and others.

Afghanistan: A Brief Summary

Afghanistan remains an impoverished, war-ravaged, land-locked country, about the same size as Texas, with a population of about 29 million (CIA 2010). But this description fails to convey the way the climate and landscape constrain the mobility of people and livelihoods or limit access for women to health and education. Almost 85 percent of the population relies on subsistence agriculture or animal husbandry. The countryside is mountainous, and many rural areas are cut off from urban centers for months at a time. Most people in rural areas travel by foot, donkey, or horseback. Before and during Taliban control of most of the country, there were few paved roads, except for one that ringed the country and linked the five major cities of Kabul, Kandahar, Herat, Mazar-e-Sharif, and Jalalabad. That road was almost totally destroyed during the fighting against the Soviet army. Cars traveled the roads, but at a pace that was barely faster than walking.

The country is home to people of many different ethnic and linguistic groups. The largest ethnic group is the Pashtuns, in both rural and urban areas, and is the same group from which the Taliban grew. The Pashtuns (also called Pakhtuns) are tribal, agrarian people who live on both sides of the

Ethnic Groups

- Aymaqs
- Nuristanis
- Baluchis
- Pamiris
- Pashaïs
- Uninhabited areas
- Pashtuns
- Hazaras
- Tajiks
- Uzbeks
- Turkmens

Durrand line—the Afghanistan/Pakistan border. The second largest groups are the Hazara (a Shia minority that live in the central highlands) and the Tajiks (ethnic Persians). Unfortunately, many warlords and some ethnic groups, including the Taliban, targeted the Hazara during the war with the Soviets and after. There are many other ethnic and language groups, as well. In spite of the many iterations of war in the country, starting with the Soviet invasion in 1979, and subsequent internal battles for power, Afghans see themselves as members of the nation of Afghanistan. Nonetheless, ethnic conflict has been on the rise, as various groups vie for power and status.

According to UN Human Development measures (United Nations 2009), which are designed to delineate the realm of choices and opportunities afforded various groups of people and then rank nations based on how their citizens access those opportunities, Afghanistan usually sits at or near the bottom on all indicators. Over half of the population is under the age of 18, and life expectancy at birth is only 43 years. This means that over half the population was born after the war with the Soviets ended. Here we find one of the worst maternal and infant mortality records in the world, though it is slowly improving. Most doctors live in urban areas, running clinics to which

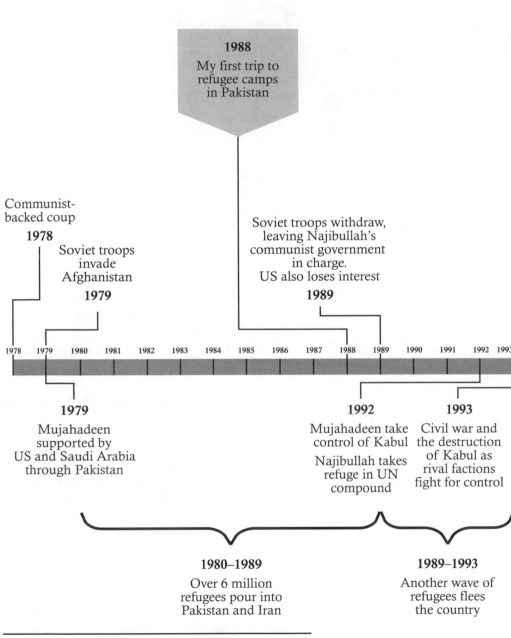

1988
My first trip to refugee camps in Pakistan

Communist-backed coup
1978

Soviet troops invade Afghanistan
1979

Soviet troops withdraw, leaving Najibullah's communist government in charge.
US also loses interest
1989

1978 1979 1980 1981 1982 1983 1984 1985 1986 1987 1988 1989 1990 1991 1992 1993

1979
Mujahadeen supported by US and Saudi Arabia through Pakistan

1992
Mujahadeen take control of Kabul

Najibullah takes refuge in UN compound

1993
Civil war and the destruction of Kabul as rival factions fight for control

1980–1989
Over 6 million refugees pour into Pakistan and Iran

1989–1993
Another wave of refugees flees the country

Timeline reflecting Afghanistan's decades of war and the author's activity in the region.

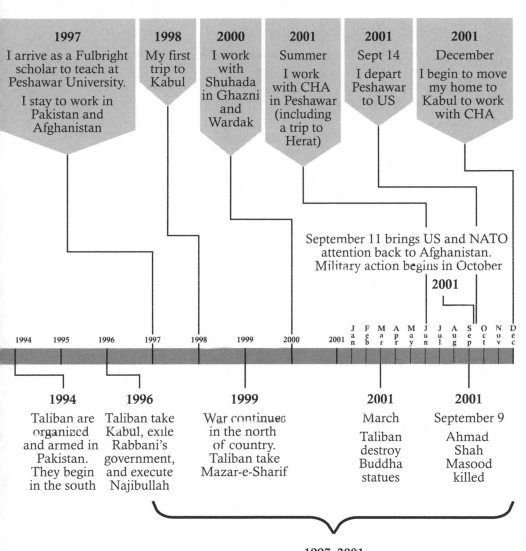

1997
I arrive as a Fulbright scholar to teach at Peshawar University.

I stay to work in Pakistan and Afghanistan

1998
My first trip to Kabul

2000
I work with Shuhada in Ghazni and Wardak

2001
Summer
I work with CHA in Peshawar (including a trip to Herat)

2001
Sept 14
I depart Peshawar to US

2001
December
I begin to move my home to Kabul to work with CHA

September 11 brings US and NATO attention back to Afghanistan. Military action begins in October

2001

1994 1995 1996 1997 1998 1999 2000 2001 J a n F e b M a r A p r M a y J u n J u l A u g S e p O c t N o v D e c

1994
Taliban are organized and armed in Pakistan. They begin in the south

1996
Taliban take Kabul, exile Rabbani's government, and execute Najibullah

1999
War continues in the north of country. Taliban take Mazar-e-Sharif

2001
March
Taliban destroy Buddha statues

2001
September 9
Ahmad Shah Masood killed

1997–2001
More refugees flee

few rural women have access. Also, many areas are so remote that communities are snow-bound for six months or more per year. Before the war with the Soviets started in 1979, life expectancy at birth was only about 52 years; during the time that the Taliban ran much of the country, this number dropped to barely over 40 for both men and women. Only about one-quarter of all babies born live to see their fifth birthday; 165/1,000 babies die at birth. Afghanistan has one of the highest fecundity rates in the world, yet few mothers survive to see old age, because most die during childbirth. The only advantage women had during Taliban time was that many women doctors fled the oppression of the Taliban in Kabul to set up clinics in rural areas, in their home villages. However, many of those clinics closed within a few months of the establishment of Hamid Karzai's post-9/11 government. At that time, the doctors returned to their urban homes and practices.

Getting health care, education, or any other aid into much of the country was a logistical nightmare during the time of the Taliban. And it has barely improved over the subsequent years. I liked to describe Afghanistan as the dream drive for enthusiasts of "off-road" jeep adventures. From Kabul to Kandahar it is only 285 miles (460 km), but the drive would take over 18 hours. That road had been destroyed during the war against the Soviets and the Soviet-backed Afghan army. Imagine trying to ship food and other aid across a country with roads that were little better than dried riverbeds—often worse. Villages that were only kilometers away were almost inaccessible. Existing roads were impassible in the winter because of the snow and were often flooded in the spring.

Afghanistan seems to be a country where one thing is constant: war. In 1989, as I worked with the Afghan refugee community in California, we celebrated the end of fighting as the Soviets withdrew, only to feel the sharp disappointment when that conflict changed to a brutal civil war. Kabul, having survived the war against the Soviets, was destroyed by the various warlords as they fought over who should rule the country. By the time I visited Kabul in 1998, whole sectors of the city were reduced to rubble. Repairs did not start until well after the Taliban left and Karzai's U.S.-backed government was in place.

The Tales I Want to Tell

In chapters 1–3, I describe various aspects of my experiences as a consultant in three areas of Afghanistan: Kabul in 1998, Hazarajat (an area in the central highlands, which I visited on two occasions) in 2000, and Herat in 2001. With each trip to these places I could feel that the Taliban were becoming increasingly entrenched, while Afghan citizens were becoming more and more rebellious. The rules constantly changed, as did the problems of travel. It was never easy to travel, whether by plane or by road, but the how and when of travel added to the totality of the experience.

The work was compelling but the needs of the Afghans were enormous. Over the years, the war shifted location and intensity. Poverty, crop loss from drought, and lack of infrastructure deepened the hardships faced by the Afghan people. By 2001, continued fighting and the drought forced large numbers of people out of their villages and into camps near cities. The Taliban, instead of allowing aid to reach these people, often harassed those who were trying to help and diverted aid to their own areas.

On each trip I felt overwhelmed by what I saw. It was not until my final trip to Herat that I had developed skills that helped me deal with my emotions and those of others around me. In working to design a mental health and psychosocial wellness program for an Afghan NGO, I discovered Focusing (Focusing Institute 2003). This is a self-help process that allows one to deal with difficult situations and emotions by holding emotions and reactions (no matter how intense) in a kind-hearted and healing way inside oneself. By the summer of 2001, I was using this practice, like a mini-meditation, daily.

In chapter 4, I describe some of the issues faced by my Afghan friends and colleagues, and myself. In chapter 5, I address my relationship to the two Afghan NGOs for which I worked. My experiences were sometimes adversarial, but mostly mutually supportive. The hardest task came when I was asked to help one of these agencies by developing a psychosocial program that would be culturally relevant and socially acceptable. That is also where I gained the most intellectually.

Next I describe my abrupt departure from the region shortly after the tragic events of 9/11, that fateful day when all our lives changed. I felt that change differently because I was evacuated from my home (in Peshawar) and exiled from my friends and colleagues. My Afghan friends knew what I was experiencing, as they lived as refugees and had themselves been uprooted without warning. While my heart went out to the families who lost loved ones that day, I found a great deal of support from Pakistani and Afghan friends and colleagues. It is hard to imagine what life might be like today had the events of 9/11 not happened. Most Afghans were (and are) thankful that the world community came to their aid and support. To this day, most have no desire to see the Taliban return or for American or NATO forces to leave.

The book ends (chapter 7 and the postscript) with reflections on the people, places, and events that are the "ingredients" of Afghanistan, comprising an unsteady concoction that challenges Afghans in their daily lives. When I ask my friends: when will peace come to Afghanistan? They answer: "When bamboo bloom"—*waqt-e-gul-e-nai*. This was a phrase I often heard when people talked of situations that were unlikely to occur. In Persian it means the same as the English phrase: "When pigs will fly." But it contains a grain of hope, because some bamboo do bloom, albeit once in 100 years. Will there be peace in Afghanistan? When bamboo bloom. Will government corruption end? Same answer. Yet, with this phrase comes a subtext. Sufi poetry, commonly quoted in Afghanistan, often refers to the bamboo/reed flute, the *nai*. Rumi's *Masnavi* opens with the story of the bamboo being pulled from their place by the river, symbolic of how humans have been pulled away from their closeness to the Divine. When one plays a bamboo flute, the air passing through it blackens the inside of the flute, as if it were burnt, in the same way the love for the Beloved (God) burns and polishes the heart of the lover. Bamboo can bloom, and there is always hope.

Chapter 1

Kabul

A Taliban Summer

Going Inside

*N*othing prepared me for my first trip to Afghanistan. Actually, nothing in my life could have prepared me for what I would experience in the place that Kabul (pronounced "cobble" like the paving stones)[1] had become under the Taliban. I had no idea what it would be like—what I would see, experience, or feel. How does one prepare oneself to work in a city that has been almost totally destroyed? And how does one prepare oneself to interact with people who have been living under an oppressive totalitarian regime? Kabul was like nothing I could have imagined. I discovered a silent city that lacked the sounds of normal urban life: no car horns, music, or children's laughter— no kites in the air or cricket matches (like in Peshawar).

As I thought back to this first trip, reread my notes and described my experiences to friends, I was struck by how much I did not understand of what I was about to encounter. Although I was an experienced traveler in Pakistan, and had worked with Afghan refugees for over 12 years in the U.S. and in Pakistan, I went to Kabul with a naïveté about the political and social situation there, and with a touch of arrogance because of the knowledge I had gained from living with an Afghan refugee family in Peshawar. In my early experiences in Afghanistan I found it difficult to emotionally manage what I saw in a more immediate way. Three years later, I had learned the method of Focusing (see the introduction) that gave me the ability to step back and view people and events without judgment. Having the capacity to do this three years earlier would have made a huge difference for me on this trip.

Getting into Afghanistan ("going inside," as we used to say) always set the stage for the trip as a whole and was its own adventure. Travel into the Kabul airport was an allegory of the political landscape of the country; the buildings and personnel reflected the changes occurring in the city and the countryside. Each trip inside was different and each landing at the airport was met with unexpected changes. Being away from the airport for more than a few months meant that one would be confronted by changes in such simple things as parking or in whether or not one pays an airport tax. Some changes literally occurred overnight—laws changing from one day to the next that forced one to miss one's flight unless an obligation was met or a bribe was paid. Other changes were slower, based on construction or on security. Under the Taliban there was little progress at the airport, only dark, dusty destruction.

Kabul by Air

My first trip to Kabul was in June 1998 when I was exploring whether I would be able to work there and be a part of the Save the Children (SAVE) U.S. team. This trip was important, as life in Kabul was restrictive for all international staff. Not everyone would be able to deal with the demands placed on them because of those restrictions, including the fact that each NGO's international staff were expected to live together in one guesthouse. It would not be easy to live and work with the same people, day in and day out.

Because I had no idea what it would be like in Kabul, the experience of traveling from Islamabad to Kabul by air set the tone for the whole trip. If nothing prepared me for Kabul under the Taliban, it is also true that nothing prepared me for the strangeness I confronted in the process of flying to Kabul. This was not a normal commercial flight. I was booked on the UN flight, the main carrier for expat staff traveling into Afghanistan at that time. My day started when a driver picked me up from my guesthouse at 6:15 AM. The previous night I asked someone at the SAVE office what to expect and how the system worked. I knew it would not be like taking a commercial flight from Los Angeles to San Francisco. She told me to be a sheep and follow everyone else. So I did.

This flight did not start at the airport but at a converted house in a wealthy residential area of Islamabad. The driver dropped me at the gate of what looked like a family home. It was the UN flight office. There, UN staff processed all travelers' baggage and documents before heading to the airport. I was a bit early and wondered if I was in the right place. It is hard to be a sheep and follow the lead of others when alone. Finally, the driveway filled with people of varying nationalities (Kenyan, American (U.S.), British, and others), all of whom worked in Afghanistan. I noticed that I was dressed differently from most of the women: like a Pakistani from Peshawar, wearing a typical *shalwar kamees* (the tunic dress over baggy pants with a tablecloth-sized cotton shawl) and sandals. In contrast, the women on this flight were wearing large, long sleeved shirts, jeans, and sports shoes. I looked colorfully Pakistani; they looked messy but comfortable.

Conversations bubbled around me as most people waiting for the flight worked together or at least knew each other. Everyone there had had a "first time," and most recognized my excited and slightly anxious expression, typical of the new kid on the block. They wanted to know who I was and why I looked so Pakistani. I had to explain to everyone that I had lived in Peshawar for the last ten months, teaching at Peshawar University, and had been conducting research on women's mental health in local villages. In turn, I listened to their stories while we waited for our luggage, including purses, to be weighed. Because of strict weight limits, we would be charged for each kilo over the limit.

At 7:30 everyone piled into one van as our luggage went into another and off we drove to the Islamabad International Airport. There we were ushered into an office, gave our passports to an airport official, and then followed him past every security checkpoint in the place.

The author in shalwar kamees and a large embroidered shawl. Peshawar 1998. (Photo by Robert Lawrence)

There was no sign of our luggage, which, I found out later had gone straight to the plane, so there were no bags to check. I have never moved through an airport faster. We even walked past diplomats. Passengers to other destinations had to move aside for us. Within ten minutes of entering the airport we were in the departure lounge, a process that usually took an hour or more.

After all the bustle and rush we were informed that the Kabul plane would be flying later than planned due to flat tires. I did not mind waiting for the tires to be fixed but was a bit anxious because I knew it was critical that we arrive in Kabul before 10:00 AM local time. There was a window of cease-fire from 9:00 to 10:00 AM. After that, any plane on or near the runway was fair game in this crazy war. At this time, fighting was fierce between the Taliban and ethnic groups from the North of Afghanistan—the Northern Alliance. Kabul came under daily mortar and rocket attack from surrounding hills, though most people in the city ignored the shelling and went about their daily affairs.

At last, we got called to board the plane and exited the building, getting on a small bus that drove us to the UN plane, parked the farthest from the terminal. In this airport, all planes were parked away from the terminal and everyone rode busses to and from their planes. I had flown many times out of Islamabad, so I was used to this procedure. But I was startled to see such a small plane—smaller than the tiny, twin propeller plane that flew daily to Peshawar. I knew the drive from Islamabad to Kabul would take at least 15 hours, and I thought that the flight would be long—yet here was a tiny twin propeller plane that held only six people. What I did not realize was that the flight time was under an hour. Kabul and Islamabad are very close, but the lack of good roads in Afghanistan made the drive long and exhausting because cars never went faster than 25 miles per hour.

We took off with a planned stop in Jalalabad, less than 100 miles from Kabul and just across the Afghanistan–Pakistan border from Peshawar. The scenery from the plane was breathtaking. I remember even now looking out the window of the plane as we flew between the mountains, whose high peaks could be seen only by looking upward. These were huge mountains almost devoid of trees. It was only when we started our descent into Jalalabad that I realized that I was finally in Afghanistan, a place I had studied for years but never thought I would see.

Once on the ground, everyone was allowed to step down from the plane and look around, while one person deplaned, along with lots of baggage. Most of the men standing around the airport looked as I had expected, the same as the Afghan men who lived in Peshawar. I saw one *talib* (one talib, many Taliban), who had the obligatory beard and large black turban. Someone told me that one could recognize the Taliban in Kabul, as they wore these turbans, looked like villagers, and thought they owned the place—even though they were usually very young.

Never mind the people, I was amazed at the rugged hills surrounding us beyond which were the high, snow-capped peaks of Tora Bora (a section of the White Mountains in which Osama bin Laden was suspected of hiding).

The mountains are so high that they keep their snow this late in the year. Picture a narrow, lush green valley surrounded by brown barren hills, with high peaks beyond them that hold up the clouds. The river provides water for crops and keeps Jalalabad alive. The city and farms are a contrast of vibrant greens, brown adobe houses, and colorful patches of laundry drying in the sun. The scenery reminded me of parts of Arizona—green in the farming areas but bone-dry everywhere else. The other thing I noticed was that, unlike the urban areas of Pakistan, there was no smog and it was very quiet.

We stayed at this airport only long enough to get the cargo off the plane and were soon off to Kabul. The pilot reminded us that we had to arrive during the time of the cease-fire—a reminder that added to the excitement I was already feeling. I was not sure when we would be landing in Kabul, but it was near the end of the "window of opportunity." We came over the mountain from Jalalabad and descended rapidly toward the airport. In the small plane we could see the landing strip out the front window as the nose of the plane pointed downward. There were no extra turns or banks and circles to ease the approach.

Once we landed, we were ushered off the plane, yet the scene was chaotic enough that many of us stood around waiting for some guidance. I found it hard to be a sheep and follow the crowd because the crowd refused to move. The crew had to load the plane for a run to Faizabad, yet they had almost no time left. They started rushing. The UN security person was hovering around the plane and could not really talk to any of us until the plane was safely on its way. This was the first feeling of unease. I was even more nervous than need be as I forgot that Afghanistan was a half-hour behind Pakistan and we had at least 20 minutes to spare. The planes don't take off or land once the window of safety closed, as no one wanted to take unnecessary risks. I learned that this was the first rule here: there was no honor in risking your own life or that of others.

We walked as a group into the terminal, to be met by turbaned, kohl-eyed[2] talibs who checked passports and luggage. I was nervous but watched as they searched luggage and opened boxes containing computers and printers being brought in for another NGO. Finally they got to me, asking me to open my bags, yet not looking at them once they were open. They never looked me in the face or wanted to see my "women's things." With barely a wave, I was on my way. Out in the parking lot, a UN van was waiting to take me directly to the SAVE office. I had arrived.

The Work

If the flight seemed new and unpredictable, the work and the situation in Kabul were even more so. This was an exploratory trip to see if I would be able to work in Kabul as the "Children-in-Crisis Adviser" for SAVE. Because of the security issues in an area that was an active war zone, I would be living and working with the same group of expats. Not only did I need to be able to do the work, I had to know if we would all be able to get along. Before going inside, I had spent a few days at the SAVE office in Islamabad, meeting staff and getting to know the goals of its programs.

I was to work on the land mine project that taught children how to avoid land mines by helping them identify the warning signs. Also, SAVE wanted solidly researched data from which to build programs that targeted real needs. At that time there were scant baseline data on the Afghan situation, particularly on how Afghan children were affected by the war. I was warned that I would have to be very flexible, because it was becoming increasingly more difficult for expats to work in Kabul, as the Taliban constantly closed programs, told foreigners to leave, and hassled those who stayed. On this trip, the director of SAVE warned me that relations between the Taliban and the NGO world had become very contentious. He was not sure if we would be able to implement any program that I designed, because, he said, "every time we develop a program the Taliban announce an edict that prevents it."

At that time, the greatest block came from the section within the Taliban called *"Amir bil Maroof wa Nahi An il-Munkir"* (The Prevention of Vice and Promotion of Virtue)—referred to as *Amir bil Maroof* or simply as the V&V— a branch of the Taliban dedicated to rooting out committers of even the smallest of infractions and then beating the unfortunates into conformity. Most V&V were young men who reminded me of thugs or members of some street gang from a B movie. They would terrorize women on the street and thought nothing of brutalizing an elderly man, an act that was in violation of Afghan cultural norms that required youth to show respect for elders. No one could complain about the actions of someone in the V&V; they had too much power.

The V&V drove around Kabul in large, extended-cab pickups, wore black turbans, and often carried long cudgels or whips. If a woman ventured into public alone, took a taxi, or went shopping, she could be beaten. But, even more likely, the V&V would beat her brother, husband, or father for her infraction. The V&V often prevented women from reaching hospitals for their jobs or in times of emergencies. Women doctors, with government permission to work, were not exempt from harassment, in part because most V&V were illiterate and could not read the document that authorized the female doctors' travel. The situation was dangerous because these edicts severely restricted women's movements, prevented them from working, and denied access to vital health care services for them and their children. NGO health workers, trying to prevent maternal mortality or reduce infant death rates, were blocked from access to and interaction with women in Afghanistan. We, the expat community, were forbidden to meet with women or enter Afghan homes.

The City

Kabul, a dusty, high-altitude desert city, was in ruins; its people lived in misery. Many trees had died from the drought or had been cut for firewood, as people struggled to stay warm through the harsh winters. The skeletons of buildings, looking more like dinosaur bones than buildings, marked the urban landscape. The destruction was visible from the plane as we landed. There were bomb craters, as well as carcasses of destroyed military and civilian aircraft surrounding the airport. We could see a bunker or two and were told the weed-filled area surrounding the runway was an uncleared minefield.

Kabul sat in the midst of high mountains, still snow-capped in June. It had the feel of western Colorado (where I grew up) because of its low humidity and elevation; both were mountain/desert areas at about 6,000 feet above sea level. I could only hope that my body would remember how to adjust. As we drove through the city to the SAVE office I realized that the road had only very light traffic. Most of the cars on the road had NGO or UN signs; only a few were taxis. I saw few people and almost no women on the street. It was hard to imagine a city of almost one million people this quiet in the middle of a workday.

Kabul was built in a fairly narrow river valley among the foothills of high mountain peaks. Roads were built around rather than over these hills. Middle- and upper-class homes were built in the flat areas along the river, between the hills. The poor built their homes on the side of the hills, climbing up treacherous paths and rocky steps to reach them. One of my friends, the cleaning woman at the office where I worked in 2004–2007, lived on the side of one of these hills. She and her daughters carried water and everything else up to their house, since no services were provided there. It was a hard climb, and once my friend's elderly sister slipped on the icy steps and broke her leg. Getting her down from the hill and to a hospital was very difficult for everyone.

Kabul Airport, 2001: bombed buildings and destroyed planes in heaps near the entrance.

Most of the houses were flat-roofed structures, made from cement blocks, with plastic covered windows. Many were abandoned but this varied by area and necessity. Before the 1979–1989 war, Kabul was a city of about 500,000 people but had swollen to over one million by 1998. It was estimated that about 40 percent of the population were internally displaced persons (IDPs)—people who had fled the fighting in their home areas and came to Kabul for safety and or work.

Later, when I was driven around the city by staff from the SAVE office, I got a closer look at the heavy destruction war had wreaked on human life and livelihood. I had been in Berlin years before when that wall came down and visited the Kaiser Wilhelm-Gedächtniskirche, whose tower was left as a memorial to the destruction of World War II. As a symbol of the destruction of Berlin, that tower had no correlation to what I viewed in Kabul—the German edifice was a memorial, while this was living devastation. The famous tombs on the hill were almost leveled, their roofs missing. The ancient Bala Hisar fort that stood above the British cantonment in the 1800s was two-thirds rubble; the palaces of former kings were irreparable shells. Only the wall of the city on the crest of the hill, built 1,300 years ago, had withstood the succession of wars here.

The destruction of Kabul occurred after the Soviets left in 1989, as the various warlords fought for control in internecine battles that left few areas untouched. Each warlord, head of a mujahadeen faction (the same groups that had fought against the Soviets in the 1980s), with his army, sat on one of the many hills in Kabul and rained rockets down on the houses below. One district near the Kabul museum, on the road to the Darulaman Palace, had once been a tree-lined avenue running through neighborhoods of wealthy homes. It then became the battleground between several rival factions and was almost completely leveled. The only people living there in 1998 were the

Darulaman Palace, Kabul, 2001. Photo was taken from the top floor. The palace was destroyed after the Soviets left Afghanistan in 1989.

A main street in
Kabul, 2001.

koochi nomads with their black tents and their herds of sheep—and the area
was littered with unknown numbers of unexploded ordnance (UXOs) and
land mines.

In the early part of the 1990s, Kabul residents moved frequently to avoid
the fighting as the various warlords struggled for control. During that time,
the front lines of the battle shifted around the city. Kabul was fought over for
more than five years after the Soviets pulled out and would, I was sure,
become a war zone again in the future. The Taliban stopped the factional
fighting in the rural areas to the south and west. But, their presence in Kabul
came with a very heavy price for the residents. To the Taliban, Kabul seemed
decadent, un-Islamic, and out of control. In addition, the ethnic groups to the
north and east of Kabul refused to cede to the Taliban, causing the war to
intensify in those areas. Just a few kilometers to the north of Kabul the battle
raged, and civilians, mostly farmers, were forced from their homes to find refuge in the city.

During this trip, I viewed a number of SAVE projects, traveling from one
area to the next, seeing more devastation, more senseless ruin. When we
passed the Olympic stadium, my guides pointed it out to me as the place
where the Taliban removed people's hands or lashed them for doing something "wrong." Finally we drove past the once famous carpet bazaar, now
completely leveled. It was an area marked for its "lasagna" mine fields, multiple layers of mines and rubble.

At the same time, I saw people hard at work trying to get on with their
lives. It was common to see shops constructed from scrap or old freight con-
tainers. In other places people had cleared out the rubble from shops that had
been bombed, put up doors, maybe a roof of plastic or scrap metal, and
reopened for business. These small shops were everywhere.

Working in Kabul

The morning I arrived, I was taken directly to the SAVE office in Shar-e-Naw (New City), a quiet, upscale residential area, not far from the airport, with expensive homes hidden behind high walls. It looked neglected; most walls and the buildings needed paint and repairs. Many of the homes in this area were converted into offices by the relatively few NGOs working in Afghanistan.

There, I was greeted by a *chowkidar* (gatekeeper) who knew excellent English and used an intercom to ask if I should be admitted. Once inside, I wandered through a lovely, well-kept rose garden to the largest building, a three-story cube of a structure that had obviously been a fine residence at one time. I could see the back area, which had a kitchen garden and a building that served as a staff training room as well as the dining room at lunch. Although there were no signs of bombings to this building, sandbags protected all ground-floor windows, bringing home the fact that I was standing in the midst of war.

I spent that first morning listening to the stories of what it was like to live and work under the Taliban. I quickly developed a great respect for all the staff, both Afghans and expats. They worked under great hardship caused in part by the many restrictions on their movements. The international women staff could not wander off to do shopping or visit friends without careful thought. All international staff shared living quarters. National male staff had to take care as they moved about the city doing their work. They could be harassed by the V&V for working with foreigners, or for not attending prayers at their home mosque, or even for having beards that were too short. Afghan women staff were forced to stay home, as an edict kept them from working with foreign agencies.

The war would feel close one moment and distant the next. It was easily forgotten, until one looked at the sandbags covering the windows or took the tour of the safety bunker, fully stocked and ready for use. Then it was forgotten again until I heard what must have been a rocket blast nearby. No one jumped but me. Destruction was normal. A young Afghan man, Qais,[3] told me that they learned to listen to the sound and could tell what kind of device it was (rocket or mortar round), if it was coming in or going the other way, and how close it was likely to hit. Generally, he said, they ignored the bombing as a normal part of their lives.

Life as an Expat in Kabul

On my first day I got my first lesson in the tension between the NGOs and the Taliban, as John, head of the Kabul office, took me to lunch at the SAVE residential compound a short drive away. As we approached the car, I immediately headed for the backseat. John stopped me and told me to sit in the front. Once in the car I learned why. Recently, a V&V squad had harassed his wife, Mary, just because Afghan men from the office had accompanied her to the bazaar. The V&V were angry that she was in the front seat with the

Afghan driver. They told Mary she had to sit in the back. She responded with a demand to see identification as proof that they worked for the Afghan government. Instead they brandished their whips. They finally stopped yelling at her and turned their ire on the unlucky Afghan driver, who was more vulnerable. When the group got back to the office and discussed the story with all the Afghan staff, everyone decided that from that day forward all foreign women should sit in front whenever possible. Other NGOs, in contrast, decided that women would always sit in the back. From that day onward, I always rode in the front, even in post-Taliban times.

The living quarters for the SAVE international staff was in a large compound on Flower Sellers Street, across the main road from Chicken Street (a famous Kabul market area), listed in the tour guides of the 1960s as the "must-see" spot in Kabul. Kabul had been one of the important stops for hippies who traveled from Europe to India. The hippies were long gone, and the tourist shops were struggling to survive on the few sales they could make to the small number of aid workers in the city. Both Flower Sellers Street and Chicken Street were semi-deserted, and most of the shops were closed. There were so few cars on the street that there was no need to walk on the sidewalk. It was a strange experience after being in overcrowded and auto-polluted Peshawar.

The house next to the SAVE compound was busy day and night with the comings and goings of talibs of all ranks and ages. It turns out that they were part of the secret police. Geri, a nurse-midwife from the United States, told me that a man from there came to our gate and asked to speak with her. He introduced himself as belonging to the secret police. I found this amusing since I had always presumed that the idea of secret police was to be . . . well . . . secret. It turns out that these very upright fellows had our compound under surveillance from their roof and felt that Geri was not dressed properly when she was at home. They were offended, or so it seemed. She pointed out the problem with the man's logic—that the Taliban forbade men from looking at women within the privacy of their home—and he went away.

For security reasons, all international staff for SAVE lived in one place and kept close tabs on each other when outside of the office. Yet, living together created its own set of problems because you ended up living and working with the same people, day in and day out, for months on end. Luckily, in the compound there were a number of ways to get out of each other's way. The area was large and consisted of several buildings. Like the office building and most homes in this part of the world, the residence was surrounded by a high wall and included a large garden area. The main house had many bedrooms, a large kitchen, a dining area, and meeting rooms.

That house was really beautiful and offered a feeling of spaciousness and roominess. It would have been light and airy had it not been for the sand bags that obscured all the ground-floor windows. The previous year a rocket had hit the kitchen. Luckily it was after the cook had gone home for the night, and no one was hurt. The sandbags had become a permanent condition of life here. The other security area I saw was the bomb shelter below the kitchen, which was equipped with enough food and water, blankets, and other supplies to last the residents for a week.

Another way to help ensure security for staff, both national and international, was the almost constant use of walkie-talkie radios. Each time I left the office or the residence compound, John was notified by radio, and when I returned someone radioed to tell him of my safe return. The two-way radio was a critically important lifeline for aid workers in war zones, especially where there is no telephone service. Staff of NGOs and the UN used radios, creating a cacophony of background noise on every channel. While working, expatriates, heads of departments, and all field staff carried radios in order to keep in touch with the office and each other at all times. These were critical as the situation in Kabul could rapidly change, making instant communication necessary. Security was an immediate concern of all staff, and it remained so even after the Taliban had left and the Americans arrived.

On the other hand, as Geri and I talked, I stated my unease at how most of the foreigners I met ignored local culture and tried to maintain their own lifestyle instead. Many seemed to act as if they were living in a bubble. On one afternoon I joined Geri at the UN Club. This was the gathering place, the watering hole for expats from all countries. I could sense an attitude of defiance here. Every Friday, expats would come here to be as Western as they wanted to be—men and women swimming, drinking alcohol, and enjoying each other's company—activities that were not practiced by Afghans. They formed a tight-knit and very small community of about 150 people who looked after each other. Most aid workers were in their 20s and early 30s and seemed to spend a lot of their free time drinking. Many of the young people I met in Afghanistan reminded me of people trying to be either "Indiana Jones" or "Rambo."

Because I wanted to understand Afghan culture, I was less willing to look at the struggle of the expat community here. I was used to living within the Pakistani and Afghan communities of Peshawar and had very little contact with expats there, so my experience with that community was very limited. What I did not appreciate were the restrictions placed on the foreigners by the Taliban and the ways expats' interactions with Afghans could hurt those very people they wanted to help. At that time, I did not realize that I was being both naïve and judgmental, or that my arrogance could lead to disaster for old friends. The edicts of the Taliban made mixing with the Afghans dangerous for the Afghans, something I did not fully appreciate until much later.

Experiencing Kabul

The next morning people at the office found out I could speak Persian, called Dari, the Afghan dialect. Unfortunately, my Dari is peppered with Iranian Farsi, giving the illusion that I speak on an educated level that I do not. Local staff began talking to me in rapid fire. Everyone was so happy that I spoke Dari that they did not consider that I was not fluent. I had to struggle to keep up. Ostad Enayat, the man in charge of the Children and War section (the department where I would work), was a scholar and lover of poetry. My ability to speak some of his language helped and we seemed to come to a quick understanding. This is where my experience with Afghans and Pakistanis paid off. Ostad Enayat and I drank tea and talked about everything from work to poetry and other interests. We got on well and he told someone later that he thought he would be able to work with me. I had been warned that this man was going to be either an ally or an antagonist, but it appeared that I had passed the first hurdle.

Usually expat staff ate lunch at their compound, but one day Geri and I joined the Afghan staff for lunch. The dining room was in one of the buildings behind the main office, next to the kitchen garden. In Afghanistan, most offices served lunch to their staff, local food that was prepared simply and with lots of oil. We were warmly welcomed. Ostad Enayat was pleased that we joined them and, so typical of the Afghans, was a very generous host.

In the afternoon, he took me to the home of one of two female community social workers in Shar-e-naw, the newer district in Kabul that had residential areas, a large shopping area, restaurants, and a gutted cinema but also looked tattered and terribly run down. Ostad Enayat told me that the women we were going to visit were doing basic social work for the social and health needs of children disabled by land mines, rockets, or UXOs. Before the Taliban edicts stopped them from working, these women were developing expertise that was desperately needed here.

When the Taliban first ordered all women out of their jobs, many women tried to visit each other in order to stay busy. Because the edict required that females travel with a male family member, this made such excursions difficult as it made women dependent on the time that other family members could give them. Many women soon gave up and just stayed home, confined to quarters that were made more stifling when the Taliban ordered all street-facing windows to be painted over with black paint—they did not want any woman accidentally seen by a passerby. If women went out, they did so in groups of three or more, and of course they wore the chadari—the garment that covered women from head to foot like a pleated sack.

When you only see the lower pant legs and shoes of a woman, you learn to pay attention to the details of anything that does show. For example, one of the ways women embellished their clothes was by varying the embroidery on the chadari or even scalloping the bottom edge, and noticing these kinds of variation became easier over time. It was interesting that no matter how hard the government tried to dictate fashion, women found ways to individualize their clothing. Even though the feet and lower legs (covered in pants under their skirts) were all that showed, there was a range and variety of choice and style. They could make statements about themselves just by the shoes they wore. I quickly learned to tell the education and social background of women by their shoes. In addition, the older women of Afghanistan usually wore mid-calf-length light-colored dresses with white pants of a light-weight fabric hemmed in lace. The younger women of Kabul tended to wear darker-colored dresses and black pants; their dresses were usually in Western styles—this had been at one time a very fashion-conscious city.

When we arrived at Shirin's house, we were brought to the sitting room reserved for guests. It was simply furnished in the typical Afghan style of red hand-knotted carpets covering the floors and cotton mats used for sitting. In this middle-class home even the bolsters upon which I leaned were carpeted. Shirin and her colleague, Zahra, who was also waiting to meet me, were trained in physical therapy, as well as social work. Furthermore, both had recently been trained by a consultant to do psychological evaluations and therapy. Frankly, I cringed at the notion that they were trying to do therapy, especially when I learned that they believed they could relieve the child's trauma in only four visits. Luckily, they were usually so busy doing social work that they had no time for psychological therapy. Indeed, for many of the children, getting their basic needs met often took care of many of their emotional troubles.

We talked for about an hour. They had no questions for me; instead they shared how they felt trapped and frustrated because they were not allowed to work. Shirin and Zahra had been assigned work in an area of Kabul that had been heavily bombed by the mujahadeen, before they were stopped by the Taliban. The Ministry of Public Health was trying to get special ID cards for all women health workers, which could be shown to the V&V when the women were stopped. It was hoped the cards would make life easier for health workers. But the man who issued the cards was traveling outside of Afghanistan, which meant that no woman could work until he returned. Meanwhile, the women sat at home hoping they would eventually be allowed to return to work. This was typical of life under the Taliban. And of course, even if the women had the cards allowing them to work, it did not mean that the V&V would actually leave them alone.

Health and Health Care

Each trip out of the office with the Afghan staff illustrated the various ways Afghans struggled to meet their community and social obligations, and the bravery with which they approached their jobs. The first afternoon that I was in Kabul, I went with the medical team—all men, of course—who conducted training sessions on disease prevention in hospitals and clinics around the city. On this day they were meeting female doctors and nurses at the maternity hospital in the center of the city.

The V&V gave only women doctors permission to work; women teachers and health educators were forced to stay home. These doctors worked, when they could get there, in government hospitals but were barred from working for foreigners. One talib in the Ministry of Public Health authorized women to work in hospitals. A doctor himself, he understood the critical need for these health care providers. But many in the V&V could not read his letters of authorization, and so many women doctors were harassed as they tried to go to work, and their female patients were blocked from getting to hospitals or clinics.

Once at the hospital, I discovered there were more Taliban orders to follow. Male doctors were not allowed in women's wards or to treat women, even in medical emergencies; health education was limited by lack of trainers and materials. Frequent new pronouncements came to circumvent all the efforts by NGOs and their staffs to accomplish any health education or reconstruction. For example, it was difficult to train health workers or their patients on how to prevent diarrheal diseases, malnutrition, or maternal and infant deaths. The Taliban's suspicious nature created a situation where NGO workers had to find ways to bend those rules without getting caught. Then the Taliban would make more rules, only to have the NGO workers find ways to break those as well. It was a constant game of cat and mouse with horrendous consequences to the aid workers and the people they were trying to help. Breaking a Taliban edict could get the health or aid worker beaten or imprisoned. Yet, following their rules meant that women would not have the critically needed health services for themselves and their children.

The SAVE health training staff often broke the rules. At this hospital they arranged to meet in a ground-floor room at the back of the hospital near a rose garden. Then they posted a guard to warn them when the Taliban came. If and when trouble arrived, the men would simply dive out the window into the garden and run away. They said it was getting harder to give these trainings because, by the summer of 1998, they were more closely watched by the V&V. And, because of the harassment of women, fewer women doctors and nurses were able to reach the hospital. These health education classes were important to the prevention and treatment of common, preventable diseases, like diarrhea and respiratory infections, as they updated the technical skills of the local staff.

Even though I knew health care delivery was a problem in Afghanistan, I was shocked at what I saw in the wards. The scene was tragic. Most of the children were suffering from various stages of severe malnutrition. In fact, at that time about 10 percent of Kabul's children suffered from chronic malnutrition, and 2 percent were severely malnourished. The SAVE staff gave doctors, nurses, and health educators training on how to do community-based prevention in order to help mothers understand the nutritional needs of their infants and children and to find ways to meet those needs in an impoverished environment. They also provided information on clinical treatment, including when to use chemotherapy. In a situation where medicine is expensive or unavailable, disease prevention through health education matters.

This was important work by very dedicated people. Yet, health education was a struggle because the health educators were not allowed to use pictures of people—one more restriction. For illiterate women (as were most Afghan women), pictures were vital to convey the health messages. The Taliban even banned pictures of hand washing. In the director's office, I was shown a poster of hand washing that was appropriate for the people in the area, because the faces of the people in the picture were blocked out. Even with this alteration, the director expected the V&V to remove this poster on their next visit.

On my third day, I went with Geri and Wahid, a friendly young man from the community health section at SAVE, to Arzan-Ghaymat (which means affordable housing), a community about 25 kilometers south of Kabul. On the drive we passed through an area that had once been served by electric buses. Wahid told me that when the communists had controlled the country, women had driven the buses, a grim reminder of how much women had lost over the years of war. As we left the city, the effects of the bombing and destruction lessened. The area we were going to was built for government workers. There was a large clinic there that served all the villages in the area. A doctor would come to give immunizations and such, but there were no permanent staff. SAVE staff did whatever health education they could for the local women and their children, but even that was limited. At Arzan-Ghaymat, the Taliban were less of a problem, though the staff stayed on the alert.

As we chatted, Geri spoke in Dari and I joined in the conversation. Wahid was surprised, as he had spent the previous afternoon with me and had not figured out how much Dari I knew. The driver also joined the discussion, deciding that my understanding of Afghan culture was good enough that I should come and stay at his home with his three wives. I asked if his wives ever fought, and he said never. (Want to bet?) We all laughed at his answer. But, he turned sad as he said that he had only a few children; most had died at birth or from childhood illnesses. The mortality rate for infants and children was very high, with over a quarter of the children dying before they reached their fifth birthday.

It was an interesting trip, and getting out of Kabul felt like a breath of fresh air. I got to know these young male health care workers and met them later, in post-Taliban Kabul, when they were having trouble adjusting to very different restrictions placed on them, as more foreigners were hired to cover expanding programs. I think it was hard for these courageous young men to shift from being independent champions of primary health care to being part of a supervised team. In Taliban times, they had gained honor and praise in taking the necessary risks to help others.

The program I was visiting was training female community health workers (CHWs) and used books like *Where Women Have No Doctors* (Burns, et al. 1997). An Afghan woman doctor, hired by SAVE as a health educator, was doing the actual training, with Geri as her supervisor. These CHWs were critical to primary health care delivery, as they were often the only health care providers Afghan women would see. On this day, the women trainees were practicing teaching on the issues of breastfeeding. I could see that Geri was a very good trainer, as she constantly asked the women in the group if the situation they were covering in the course had ever happened to them. If someone said yes, she would ask the woman what she had done. Geri always encouraged ways that were sound, even if they were new to her.

On Land Mines and Land Mine Education

On another day, I saw more of the city as I visited the land mine education programs (LEPs). We traveled to Karte Naw, District 8. This community had also been destroyed and was carpeted with the remains of bombed-out buildings. We arrived at an LEP class in progress at a mosque, the only structure that appeared to have been rebuilt. None of the windows had glass panes, instead they were covered with plastic that rattled and flapped in the wind.

My arrival was greeted by a rush of dusty children who crowded around me, staring with curiosity. There were children everywhere, and Hamed, one of the young men who supervised the local trainers for LEP, instructed them to sit quietly next to the wall. They did while he was watching them, but they immediately got up and followed me as soon as he turned his back. I felt like the Pied Piper. The children were well behaved but curious. The girls' long hair looked like it had never been brushed; their ill-fitting clothing, once colorful, was faded with age and dirt. The boys had shaved heads and wore clothing that had been either mended many times or just left ragged. All the children had quickly rinsed their faces before coming to the class, and I could see where the water made streaks as it ran down their dusty necks.

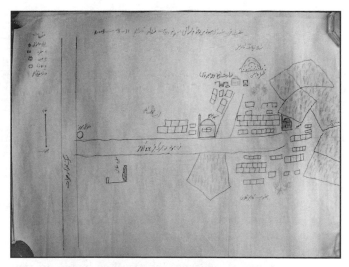

When conducting village surveys, the survey teams often worked with the community to draw maps of local resources. This map, from a village near Kandahar, is an example of community mapping and shows an active mine field at the edge of the village. Photo taken during a survey for UNICEF in 2002.

Karte Naw had been another frontline area in the battles between the warlords and had many land mines and UXOs. Although most of the land mines had been cleared, there were still many injuries as people accidentally came across one on their land or found them while scavenging for wood or metal. Most deaths and injuries in 1998 in Kabul were from UXOs.[4] The economy here had collapsed, forcing many children and men to collect scrap metal and sell it to support their families. The metal in UXOs and land mines had value, but only if it was separated from the other materials. The usual method was to open the shell and toss the innards, keeping the metal for profit. Most explosions occurred when people tried to pry open the shell. Although our job was to teach children not to do this kind of work, poverty forced them to ignore the risks. Many died while trying to earn money to feed their families, but if they did not collect the metal, they risked starvation.

Surprisingly and luckily the Taliban did not stop land mine and UXO education programs for children, as they had stopped other health programs (like tuberculoses control and diarrhea prevention). I never understood why one type of public health program was allowed to continue while the others were stopped. Perhaps the Taliban's tolerance related to the fact that men (not women) who had lost limbs from mine explosions taught many of these classes, which were often held in mosques, places that the Taliban held in high esteem.

Children and Play

In war zones, children need safe areas for playing unstructured games. In Kabul they also needed mine-free local play areas. Each day I would see new playgrounds that were built by SAVE. The agency was also encouraging the formation of soccer and volleyball teams and tournaments. These were vital for the long-term physical and emotional health of children and their families. Other agencies also had programs for children.

My final day in Kabul, Friday (a day off in Afghanistan and in many Muslim countries), started early with a trip to Khairkhana, a primarily middle-class district in the northwest corner of Kabul. John and I were going to watch a soccer game. We left the compound at 5:30 AM. I kept asking John to stop at Starbuck's for a cafe latté, but he only laughed. This was not a city of restaurants or coffee shops. We traveled through a very empty city, arriving at a patch of ground that had been cleared for soccer and volleyball; it even had an area with playground equipment for younger children.

I was glad I came, as this was the only area of the city I had seen that was intact—run down but intact. It had hardly been bombed and I saw very few other signs of fighting. I would return here with the staff of CHA in December 2001 to enjoy a shopping trip. This area felt friendlier and less "traumatized" than other sectors I had visited. The district commander, a talib, had promised John that he would be responsible for security and that all the foreign women who wanted to come would be welcome. This was not the norm for the Taliban but was typical of Afghan hospitality.

We came expecting a game between young boys and were disappointed to find that the players were all adults, although there were lots of kids watching. The men were playing hard, clearly enjoying themselves, so it was fun to relax and enjoy the event. It soon became clear, however, that the children were busy watching me instead of the game. They were so distracted that a stray ball hit one of them. My dark hair and slightly olive complexion would have allowed me to pass as a local. John, on the other hand, was fair skinned with very light blond hair. Yet, the children were more interested in watching me, the strange middle-aged woman at a public event, than the blond man. I was, after all, the only woman in sight.

I had as much fun trying to talk to the kids as I had watching the dust fly out on the soccer field. The boys standing behind me were talking about John and me. They determined that we were *Kafir* (unbelievers, non-Muslims). They believed their language was linked to Islam and were amazed that I knew some Dari. They kept talking about us, even when I replied to them, and I could barely keep from laughing. I translated for John every chance I got. The boys actually never really figured out that I could understand them. Kafirs don't speak their language: that was all there was to it!

Departure

Leaving Kabul by air was as unique as my arrival. The trip began at the International Committee of the Red Cross (ICRC) office, where the bags were processed. Everyone on the flight was taken in ICRC vans to the airport where we were again quickly processed and allowed to board the plane. This time I was carrying more luggage, thanks to a shopping spree on Chicken Street. I had bought three hand-blown Herati glasses for less than a dollar, a koochi dress with wide embroidered borders, and a yoke of heavy embroidery for next to nothing. Coming to Kabul, my luggage weighed 7 kg, but it weighted 20 kg on my return. I was asked to pay for the difference, and my inexpensive purchases ended up costing dearly.

We finally boarded the very small twin-propeller plane for the flight to Peshawar. The flight itself was bumpy because of air pockets. The mountains were spectacular, and, even though I had seen them just a few days before, I was ready to see them again. Unlike the arrival into Kabul, the landing in Peshawar was one of ease. We circled and came in at a nice comfortable rate. Once on the ground, our small group stood by the plane while the person in charge got the next party ready to leave. The plane was flying back to Afghanistan, this time to the earthquake zone in the north. It was carrying supplies for the relief work there and only a few people. We watched the ground staff remove five rows of seats to accommodate the cargo. Then we were escorted into the airport passport area and were quickly checked through. Again, we had no delays. Once out of the airport, a van took us to the ICRC office close to my home. I was dressed like a local and no one looked twice at me. After experiencing the restrictive rules of the Taliban, Peshawar felt like home, a place where I could walk in public—so I did. I walked home.

The author wearing a traditional Afghan dress, purchased in Kabul in 1998.

Reflections

Afghans are resilient, even to the point of defiance. They manage to live under almost impossible circumstances and maintain their culture and their dignity. I was amazed at the level of resilience to the situation; in the end, however, what choice was there for the Afghans living under the Taliban? Women were denied health care and education and were confined to their homes. The men were frustrated and hated the restrictions. They resented the way the Taliban forced a way of life on them that they did not recognize or accept. The young men in the research office were defiant and took amazing risks for their job.

On this trip, I also learned a lot about myself, but it took years for it to sink in. I was immediately aware of the level of caring and kindness that Afghans reach in their relationships with friends and family, and especially for their guests. I was profoundly affected by what I saw. Back at my home in Peshawar, I felt nervous and tried to contain my feelings. Kabul was overwhelming in many ways, and I finally had to take time to cry a while. Could I work there? I thought so. But I realized right away that I would need many breaks. The life was intense, and I would be working with very needy people.

On my last day in the office, I went to each room and said goodbye to everyone I had met. Everyone told me that they hoped I would be back to work with them. But I never returned to that office, even though I took the SAVE position. Before I was able to join them in Kabul, the Taliban kicked all the expatriates out of Afghanistan. SAVE relocated its expatriate staff to Islamabad. Some, like Ostad Enayat, left Afghanistan shortly after this and resettled in Europe. I met Wahid again in Kabul when I was working on a short project for SAVE in 2003. He later moved on to a new job and new possibilities. Last I heard, he was still in Kabul. I met Qais in 2007 at a Dead Sea Resort in Jordan, where we were both attending a UNICEF workshop on adolescents. He was employed by UNICEF and based in Somalia at that time. I lost touch with all the expats.

I returned to Afghanistan several times during the next few years, visiting other areas under Taliban control, but did not spend time again in Kabul until December 2001, after the Taliban left. When I came back, the city seemed to have grown even more ragged and frayed. In the winter of 2001, without the oppression of the Taliban, one could feel the collective relief in the air and in people's actions. When I walked through the bazaar in Khairkhana without my head covered, women came up to me, removed their chadaris and asked me to join them in their homes for tea. Women, men, and children all celebrated the removal of the oppressor and hopes were high. Those hopes have been slowly fading over subsequent years.

thought back on it as the easiest part of the trip. Here we sped along at about 50 kph for the hour-and-a-half ride to the border. Because I was traveling with two men, Engineer Muslim and Aziz, we had to hire two taxis. This had less to do with the size of the taxis, which were small, and more to do with the fact that the government required us to take two Kalashnikov-toting soldiers with us for our protection. I wondered if they were there to guarantee that we were actually going to the border and not off on some drug-running or smuggling expedition, as they did not look like they would be much protection should the need arise.

A slight man, balding, with a very wispy beard and mustache, Aziz was an easy traveling companion, and he took great care of me. He became one of my most trusted friends, and I quickly developed great respect for him. Trained in accounting while working for an American company before the war, he was one of the brightest people I met, though not university educated like others in his own family. He was a self-taught computer genius with a gift for language translation between Dari, Pashto, and English. He also knew some Russian, as I learned years later when we attended a peace conference in St. Petersburg. Aziz was not a friend of the Taliban and had been imprisoned and tortured by them. But he seemed fearless and could speak angrily to a talib when provoked. Luckily for us, he had been raised in Helmand, a Pashto-speaking area, and was fluent in the local Pashto dialect, which helped whenever we were stopped or questioned.

Aziz and Engineer Muslim at the Shuhada hospital in Wardak in 2000.

My other companion, Engineer Muslim, was the logistics officer and a former general under the communist-backed government; he had received training in Moscow. He also spoke Dari, Pashto, and Russian, but limited English. He seemed to be a teddy bear of a man, with his fluffy, disheveled hair, bushy beard, and stout body. It was hard to picture him as a general, though I now have pictures of him in full uniform, after he took his place in the Karzai government's army. I met him first through a Novib-sponsored gender-training program that was held in Peshawar the previous spring. We had just completed a group activity that was designed to raise awareness of just how much unpaid and unrecognized work women did in Afghan homes, as well as the ways they contributed to their families' economy. Engineer Muslim sheepishly raised his hand to say he was embarrassed to admit that he had never realized how busy his wife was in her day-to-day life. They had many children, and he said he would come home from work and expect a cup of tea to be ready, almost before he sat down. He had never considered how busy his wife had been.

On this trip, I had no idea what to expect, nor did I know the stories of those with whom I would be traveling. I discovered that ethnicity mattered, and their life history stories affected the choices they would have to make on the two journeys I made with them into Afghanistan. Yet, I did not understand, until much later, why they made the decisions they did. I also learned that it was not only cheaper for Shuhada to send me into Afghanistan, rather than bring a large group to Quetta, but because of problems between the Taliban and the Hazara people, it was safer for them, as well. Each time they traveled to a new area (outside of Hazarjat), and particularly when they tried to leave Afghanistan, they could be beaten or jailed or killed by the Taliban. The enmity between the Sunni Taliban and the Shia Hazara was brutal, with devastating consequences to the Hazara. I knew that I had to be careful and try not to draw attention to myself. As a foreigner, it was unlikely that the Taliban would hurt me, but they could easily take their resentment out on my companions.

As in all my other trips, even dress became an issue. Since I had been in Kabul before, I felt confident that I was dressed appropriately. Instead of the usual Pakistani dress of a long tunic top over baggy pants, known as the shalwar kamees, I put on an Afghan-style black dress (full skirted and without the side slits that Pakistan tops have) and pants, with a large white cotton shawl, called the *chador*, which covered my hair and most of my upper body. Yet, Aziz was concerned that I still looked too obvious. He was nervous that I would attract attention to our team, but I could not wear the all-encompassing chadari or burqa, because the Taliban wanted a clear distinction between foreign women and Afghans. That would have gotten us in deeper trouble, as they might claim that I was spying on them. Aziz was so nervous about my shawl that he bought a large (eight-person tablecloth size) black shawl for me when we got to Kandahar.

We reached the border at Chaman without incident and left the taxis on the Pakistan side. After getting my exit stamp, we walked past the metal bar-

Kandahar was rugged and dry, littered with the bombed-out shells of tanks and other metal objects. The hill in the background has a small shrine, called "Forty Steps," carved out of the stone. Photo taken in 2002.

rier into Afghanistan. Although there were people leaving Pakistan, like us, to travel into Afghanistan, most of the foot traffic was going the other way. On the Afghanistan side, the road was filled with people trying to go to Pakistan—refugees who looked dusty, tired, and thirsty. Most of those who were denied entry could be easily identified as Hazara, the men with their thin beards and Asian faces—like Aziz. Even the Pakistan border police discriminated against them and demanded money before allowing them entry. Other Afghans, such as the Pashtuns who share ethnicity with their Pakistani neighbors and the Taliban, moved freely across the border. Another striking difference I noticed was that the rural Pashtun and nomadic Koochi women were able to travel in public without the chadari; they wore the large locally made shawl, instead. All other women were hidden under the ubiquitous chadari.

Once on the Afghanistan side of the border we quickly found a taxi (only one this time, as we had no need or desire for guards) to take us to Spin Baldak, the next town. There, we would have to find yet another taxi to take us to Kandahar. We were not traveling, as many NGO staff did, by official car; rather, we traveled as discreetly as possible by local transport. Official cars were often stopped at Taliban check posts, while local taxis were usually, though not always, ignored. Shuhada had already lost one pickup to the Taliban, and its staff were often harassed when stopped.

The road to Kandahar looked like a lunar landscape, where the mountains rose jaggedly, straight up from the level plain. Unfortunately, we could barely see them, because the air was so dusty, due to the drought that had plagued the area (see map). There were black tent homes of the Koochis everywhere, thousands of them dotted across the plains. The markets we passed were filled with their livestock, and on the plains many more animals were marked for sale. Yet, there seemed to be no grass left in this whole region for the animals to eat—just broad, dusty, empty plains that led up to

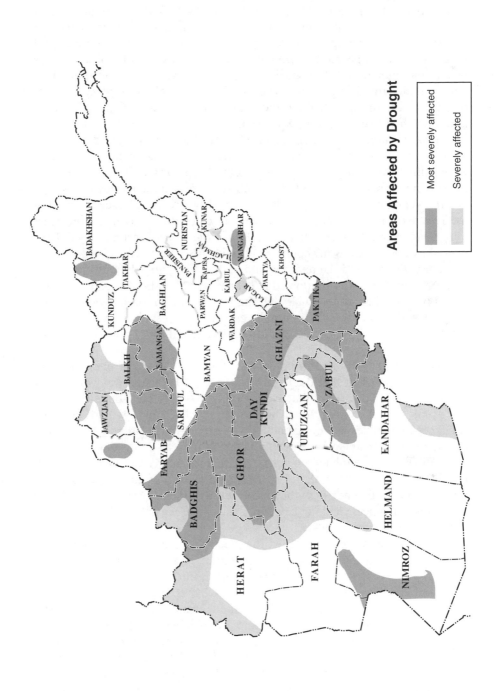

Areas Affected by Drought

Most severely affected

Severely affected

BADAKHSHAN

ITAKHAR

KUNDUZ

BALKH

SAMANGAN

BAGHLAN

PANJSHER

NURISTAN

KUNAR

KAPISA

NANGARHAR

BAGHLAN

LAGHMAN

PARWAN

KABUL

KHOST

WARDAK

LOGAR

PAKTYA

JAWZJAN

SARI PUL

BAMYAN

GHAZNI

PAKTIKA

FARYAB

GHOR

DAY
KUNDI

ZABUL

BADGHIS

URUZGAN

HERAT

FARAH

HELMAND

EANDAHAR

NIMROZ

high dusty mountains. Because of the glut of animals on the market, prices had dropped. The herdsmen had little chance of selling these animals, which would not survive the drought. I could not have imagined a place so dry and desolate (and I grew up in the deserts of Colorado). There were miles and miles of displaced people and animals, and there was no way those animals would find enough to eat by grazing. The owners were too poor to buy fodder for their large herds, if one could find any for sale. Overgrazing, combined with the drought, had left the countryside denuded. Family fortunes, tied up in their livestock, were destroyed.

It was an unimaginable sight as we bounced over horribly bad roads, the driver swerving around huge potholes, narrowly missing oncoming cars that were going toward the border. We held on to keep our seats, though we were not driving more than 30 kph (18 mph). I soon missed the bumpy roads near Quetta. When we arrived at Spin Baldak the driver seemed happy to be rid of us. This taxi driver did not like our company, nor did my companions trust him. I had been told not to talk, and if I did I was to use Dari, as they did not want the driver to know my country of origin. Also, by staying quiet, I would seem less foreign, and the driver would be less likely to ask questions about us or our purpose. In addition, the Taliban could indiscriminately punish taxi drivers for infractions, including the transport of a foreign woman who was not with her *mahram*[6] (legal male escort). The less the driver knew the better for everyone. We quickly got out and searched for another taxi to take us to Kandahar.

The cost for taxis had to be paid in Afghanis, local currency that had devalued to the point that the largest banknote, 10,000Afs, was worth only about 14 cents. This meant that everyone had to carry huge bundles of cash to buy the simplest thing. Later, when I lived in Kabul, I would hand the shopkeepers bundles without counting. They would measure the thickness of the stack to estimate value. It would take too long to count out $50 in Afs (over 350 bills). The men wore vests over their garments that had huge inner pockets to stash their bundles of money. Although Aziz and Engineer Muslim carried a sizable box of money for expenses, at least here we were able to use Pakistani rupees, making payment easier ($50 was about 2,000Rs—two 1,000Rs-denomination bills).

Once in Kandahar, we located the place for taxis that could take us to Jaghori. There was not a central transport area for all inter-city destinations, instead one had to find the particular location in the city for taxis or buses that would take you where you wanted to go. My companions wanted someone who was also Hazara to take us into the Hazarajat area. It took us only a short time to locate the right place and to secure a taxi to take us onward. By now it was mid-afternoon, and we would make no more stops in Kandahar, not even to eat. We quickly left the city behind. The only purchase was the black shawl I described above. It was clear that Aziz and Engineer Muslim were more relaxed, as they trusted this new driver. It meant that I could now talk and ask questions.

A Trail of Mango Skins

One of the delights of the trip occurred in part because I am a vegetarian and also because of the desire to avoid most roadside restaurants. Stopping long enough to eat would give locals a chance to notify the Taliban that a foreign woman was traveling with some Hazara men. But we also wanted to avoid the restaurants because it was too easy to get food poisoning, a common problem at these roadside stops. We could not afford to get sick.

In order to manage the trip, Aziz decided that we would live off of mangoes and water during our drive. If all went as planned, we would arrive in Jaghori sometime in the middle of the night, with no need to stop for food. I had already decided that mangoes are God's gift to anyone who puts up with the heat of Pakistani summers. The hotter the weather, the sweeter the mangoes become. Temperatures usually hover well above 110°F/43°C for several months in central Pakistan; the mangoes love it, and I love mangoes. Aziz froze a number of 1.5 liter bottles of mineral water, loaded them into a large carton, and filled the rest of the box with mangoes. It was enough to last us for the long trip. Engineer Muslim took charge of the supplies (he was head of logistics, after all) and doled out the mangoes and water from his place in the backseat. I sat in the front and had to do nothing but wait for a mango to appear over my shoulder from the seat behind me.

The other thing to know about mangoes is that they are very messy to eat. Whenever I ate them, I usually had to wash my hands and face, and sometimes my clothing afterward. On this trip, Aziz taught me a way to stay clean while eating a mango. It was simple; he took the mango and slowly squeezed it from the outside until the whole fruit was soft and squishy and had the feel of a water balloon. At that point, he would poke a small hole in one side and squeeze the pulp out into his mouth. No muss, no fuss. All that was left was the skin and the seed inside. We tossed those out the windows. I felt a bit like we were Hansel and Gretel, leaving a trail that would help us find our way back.

With the water, I was a bit more cautious and tried not to drink very much. On these long trips I quickly learned not to stay hydrated. There were almost no toilets, and those at restaurants were filthy. It was nearly impossible for women to find places to relieve themselves along the barren roads. Afghan women are very discreet about matters of the toilet, even to the point of not entering a toilet facility if men are standing nearby. When there are several women traveling together they can use their large shawls to form a tent within which one person hides, but I was alone. The Afghanistan terrain was fairly bare, with few trees or large rocks to hide behind. And the rocks we found often had a village on the opposite side, so there was still no privacy. In addition, the road had a fair bit of traffic, so I could not hide behind the car, either. Nonetheless, I finally got too desperate to care, and about this time, we came to one of the few bridges that had not been destroyed in the war. I thought this would be my only option.

It seemed like the perfect solution until I remembered the problem of land mines. At that time Afghanistan was one of the most heavily land-mined countries in the world. With more land mines than people, this was a major hazard for people and animals. And there were no maps to show where they had been placed. As mentioned previously, Kabul had many lasagna mine-fields. Moreover, the countryside was scattered with them, and they caused horrible injuries or death to children as they searched for firewood or herded their goats and sheep.

My dilemma was that we were traveling in a desert area known for flash floods, which could wash mines out of the hills, where they settled, buried and unseen, in the soft sands of ravines or under bridges. I had been warned about the dangers of such areas, but I was also desperate. I climbed down under the bridge, stepping only on the tracks made by sheep. As I climbed back up to the road, a bus was stopping to let some women out for the same purpose. Because I had returned safely they were ready to follow my tracks. Afghanistan needed rest stops!

The road was almost impassable. As it had been bombed so many times, it had craters instead of potholes, big enough to lose a car. Here we averaged only 10–12 mph/20 kph. Few bridges were left, forcing cars to leave the road area to drive down into the ravines, on dried riverbeds, before going back up the other side. It was an off-roader's dream drive, but it left us dusty and exhausted. I could only sympathize with our driver, who had to wrestle the car around the various obstacles, all the while trying to avoid oncoming traffic, which was busy avoiding the same obstacles. I noticed that no matter which direction one drove, the other side of the road was always smoother. One long section of the road was like traveling over large ocean waves, undulating up and down in a series of crests and troughs that went on for miles. I thought of the washboard roads that were near our farm, where I grew up as a kid, but those roads did not compare to what we experienced here. Oddly enough, driving was easier where the road was completely gone; in those areas we drove over smooth sand.

On top of the discomfort of the rough road, we had to keep the windows open because of the heat. That left us breathing a very fine dust, similar to fine talcum powder. My black shawl and what showed of my hair quickly became grey and then white from the powder. There was a constant gritty taste in my mouth, but I did not want to drink water for fear of needing to find another toilet.

Traveling Together

By late afternoon our driver was exhausted and needed to rest. Aziz's plan of not stopping to eat did not take into account the fact that our driver would need a break. Near the turnoff that we would take to Jaghori, we came across a roadside restaurant. Many taxis and trucks were pulled up around it, and ours joined the pack. Here we could get out to eat, use the toilet (a latrine in the back that had not been cleaned in years), and stretch.

The adobe building consisted of a large room, like a wide hall down the middle of the building, with washbasins along one wall, and a row of small rooms for families (women would not eat in open, public areas) on the opposite side. We opted, of course, for one of the rooms. It was about six feet by eight feet with a window on the wall across from the door that opened out toward the road. This was covered with heavy velvet curtains. The room itself was a raised platform, about two feet higher than the floor of the common room, with a red machine-made carpet on the floor, mats to sit on, and a bolster each, upon which we could lean. It was an all-purpose room used for both dining and sleeping.

We left our shoes outside the door of our room and got comfortable. It was a relief to stop moving for a while. After the constant swerving and jostling of the drive, my body craved stillness, yet it felt like it was still moving. I could feel the room moving under me, a sure sign of fatigue. The air was cool and I could have easily fallen asleep. It would have been a relief to spend the night there. The driver wanted to stay and continue on in the morning. He let us know that he was unfamiliar with the back road to Jaghori.

But Engineer Muslim had other ideas. He took charge and said we would drive all night if need be. Not the best plan, as it turned out. He used me as the excuse, telling the driver that we could not stay here, as the three of them did not have the ability to protect me. I was a novice at this and took him at his word. When I travel I depend on local staff to keep me safe, and I prefer always to do as they suggest. It always feels better in the end to err on the side of caution. Once, years before on a visit to a refugee camp near Quetta, I did not listen to the person who was my guide, and, because of my actions, she lost her job. Since that time, I have tried to make fewer ripples so that everyone feels more secure.

When we had eaten and were ready to continue our drive, the driver discovered another van traveling the same direction. The other driver convinced ours to take another back route that was even shorter. We were optimistic until we realized that, because the other man knew the way, he drove very fast (for Afghanistan). As darkness quickly fell, the road disappeared. I could not understand how they found the road in the daytime, much less at night. After about an hour of this madcap race in the dark, the van stopped to let us know he was going a different direction and shouted instructions to our driver on how to proceed. Off we went on our own, over what appeared to be a dry riverbed. As if possessed, our driver kept the same breakneck pace as before. We continued bouncing over the road/riverbed for at least another hour. Then we were forced to stop, because the undercarriage of our car had run over a large rock that tore something lose. Our valiant Toyota could go no further.

We had no idea where we were or how much farther it would be to the next town. It was now about 11:00 PM on a moonless night. We could hear a dog barking in the distance, so we knew there were households nearby, though we did not know anything about who the people were or to which ethnic group they belonged. We could see the outlines of a large, walled structure in the distance and noticed that we were parked near a small building that appeared to be a shrine of some kind. Our driver thought we were still in a Pashtun/Taliban area and said we needed to be very cautious. Because the ethnic problems had been increasing in the region and I was traveling with members of an ethnic minority that was almost hated by the Taliban, we could not be sure how those living in this area would react if we knocked on their door in the middle of the night; nor could they take the chance to trust us. It was a wartime situation, after all.

We decided to stay put and bed down for the night. I slept in the car and my three male companions put blankets on the road around the car, both to protect me and because the road, such as it was, was softer soil than the rocky verge. After about four hours of light sleep, dawn came and we saw that our immediate neighbor was indeed a shrine—a mud-brick building that housed a tomb covered in green cloth. And with the early morning, various people came to pay their respects at the shrine and to touch the large stone that stood at one side of the building like a sentinel. My field notes described the stone as "sticking out like a sore thumb." Everyone who came to the tomb to pray stopped to kiss the top of the stone.

Aziz walked to a nearby house, less than a kilometer from us, to ask for water. He came back to tell us that we had arrived in Hazarajat and were safe.

The shrine at the side of the road where our taxi broke down. The rock that visitors kissed is visible between the two trees. Photo taken in 2000.

What a relief! I could see the group visibly relax. He also found out that this area was hard hit by the drought. The house he visited had two wells but one was already dry. Yet the family welcomed us and invited us to come inside. We decided not to because we needed to figure out how we were going to reach our destination. While Aziz went one way, Engineer Muslim decided to follow the road—it was a road not a riverbed, after all—to the nearby village. I waited at the taxi with the driver, who was trying to find a way to make repairs. As it turned out, we were within a mile of the town and had not known it. There, Engineer Muslim found us new transport, another Toyota station wagon. Very soon, we had transferred all our gear to the new taxi. We left the other poor driver behind, though he now had U.S. dollars in his pocket for his efforts. He felt he would have his car repaired very quickly and would return to Kandahar, with paying passengers. All in all he had made a profit.

My companions and I headed off toward our destination, only another three-hour drive. The road was no better, but the drive was beautiful and our spirits were upbeat as we neared our destination. The road climbed steadily upward. The mountains around us were huge and, as in other areas, totally devoid of trees. The only green we saw were the trees along the streams that came down from the high hills around us. A type of birch, these trees were used as poles in the construction of houses and constituted an important source of income for their owners. Unfortunately, I saw many trees that looked green and alive until I touched the leaves, only to have them crumble in my hand. The drought here seemed unpredictable. One village had no water and all their trees were dead, while a neighboring village still had enough water to keep theirs alive.

As we came over the last hill into Jaghori, I saw a small town dominated by a large grey building that was the Shuhada Hospital. Some 30 minutes later we pulled into the hospital compound, where we were met with enthusiasm. The doctors and heads of the education sector had been waiting for us for several days—from the time I had been waiting in Quetta. Many were anxious to return to their work and families. We arrived dusty, tired, and hungry, but started the workshop immediately after a hastily organized breakfast of local bread (naan), cream and sugar. We had a lot of work to do to plan the upcoming survey—with regard to both its content and its logistics. No one wanted to wait for us to rest, even though we had been traveling for the past 24 hours and were tired. Problems of travel were normal here; what was important was that we arrived.

Jaghori, Ghazni Province

Jaghori is both the name of the town and of its district in Ghazni Province—at an elevation of about 5,000 feet. Ghazni Province has a mix of ethnic groups, with Hazara living in the northern and western sections and Pashtuns living predominately in the southern and eastern sectors. Koochi nomads, Pashto speakers, also move through this region, though mostly in the eastern quadrant. The Koochi groups often have conflicts when they are in the settled Hazara areas, as the two groups compete for limited resources.

Hazarajat was not an easy place to visit not only because of the difficulty in getting there but also because of the status of the Hazara people under Taliban rule. It soon felt oppressive, like a land under occupation by an enemy army. Although there were Hazaras who worked for the Taliban (recruited from the local population), for the most part, those in charge were ethnic Pashtuns. In part the conflict stemmed from sectarian tension, as the Hazaras were Shia Muslims and the Taliban were Sunni. There was also a long history of conflict and subjugation of the Hazara by the ruling elites, who were also Pashtuns. This led to resentment between the Hazara and their neighbors, as well as to misunderstandings about the Hazara by outsiders. The animosities had begun centuries ago.

There were those within the Taliban who did not care if the Hazara people survived and, in fact, preferred that they did not. On the trip to Jaghori we drove past an area of cliffs and caves where I was told the Taliban had dumped the bodies of Hazaras whom they had killed. More personal to me, the Taliban had imprisoned Aziz in Helmand just a few years before. Although relations between the Taliban and local Hazaras were quite strained, relations between the Hazara and the neighboring Pashtun families were not always as contentious. At one point, the Taliban tried to starve the Hazara by setting up a food blockade around the whole region. Many Pashtun neighbors defied the blockade and smuggled food into the region so that people would not starve. Maybe they did it for the money—as it was lucrative—but it was also dangerous and they took a big risk. Because of Pashtun neighbors, the Hazara survived the Taliban blockade.

A huge, grey structure that contrasted sharply with the local buildings, the Shuhada hospital at Jaghori had 50 beds and was the largest building in the area; it seemed larger than the town itself, in which most of the buildings were constructed from stone that was covered in a mixture of mud and wheat chaff; thus, the buildings were the same light tan color as the ground on which they were built. The hospital served an extensive area; that is, many patients and their families had to travel for days by foot or donkey to get there. The place had the only electricity in town from a generator that was turned on each evening for about two hours, or during the day when a doctor needed it—for surgery or to take x-rays.

Next to the hospital was a walled compound that became my home for the next two weeks. This was a large area on the side of a low hill. Rooms were built on the inner perimeter of the high outer walls: some for guests, others for storage. A few rooms, like mine, were painted—the lower half blue and the upper portion white. Others were left unpainted. The ceilings were made in layers, starting with a base of lodge-poles that supported what looked like reeds, which were laid out neatly across the poles. Above all of this was mud mixed with straw. Each summer the roofs had to be repaired to

Jaghori, Ghazni, 2000: a view of Shuhada Hospital, taken from inside the visitors' compound.

prevent leaking. Every night I listened to mice or other creatures nibbling away at the roof and worried that something might land on me. I did not want to know what was sharing my room.

My room was along the back wall of the compound, while the men were on the opposite side of the area, giving me all the privacy I needed. It had no furniture, but there were mats on the floor for sitting and sleeping. Attached to the room I slept in was another one for bathing, a simple room that had a hole in the floor near the back wall that allowed the water to run outside. There were nails in the wall to hang clothing and my bag of toiletries. The only toilet was in the Hospital. Each morning I would try to get up early enough to get to the toilet before patients or others would start to arrive. Back at my room I could wash up from the bucket of water left for that purpose by a cleaning woman who looked after all my basic needs. She would come daily to clean my room and bring me buckets of hot water for bathing when I asked. I had trouble understanding her dialect but soon learned she had been recently widowed and was very poor.

Dealing with the Taliban

At first I was relieved to have arrived and get to work. I was excited that I would be conducting a survey in this area and would have a chance to visit homes, schools, and clinics. But I quickly became aware of the reality of the situation for those with whom I was working. A few days after my arrival, Aziz came to my room, where I was relaxing after the day's work, to tell me I needed to dress in my most conservative clothing and come for an interview with local Taliban officials. They had gotten word that a foreigner had come to the area and wanted to verify who I was and why I had come. Because we were in the midst of planning the health survey, we had been putting our thoughts on large sheets of paper and hanging them on the walls of the room where we worked. Luckily we had only worked on the health survey; we did not want them to know about the education survey.

Waiting for me in our training room were two talibs, both Pashtuns. The younger man, his eyes outlined with kohl, making them look darker and fiercer, seemed to be in charge. He started the interview and asked many questions about our work and our purpose there. The other man, older and educated, did not talk at first. I was asked to prove I had permission to be in the country and showed them my permits. The younger man took them, but we realized he was illiterate when he held the document upside down. The older man took the paper and read it out loud, verifying that I did, indeed, have permission to be in Jaghori. They wanted to know my travel plans, but Aziz was reluctant to tell them anything.

Aziz spoke in Pashto, without translating for me, only explaining the conversation later. I did not need translations to know that we were in a dangerous situation. I trusted Aziz to handle things. I was so thankful that we had not put any education posters on the walls, or we could have endangered everyone and all the programs. The conversation remained calm, and the older man asked me many pointed questions about psychology. As the discussion was ending, the younger man told Aziz and Engineer Muslim that he and his colleague were there to find corruption so that the Taliban in the area could make an example to the people by hanging anyone who cheated the poor people. They were adamant that we expose all who were corrupt in the agency—a demand we decided to ignore.

As they stood to leave, the younger man told us that I was not allowed to leave the hospital and grounds for any reason unless I did so with a talib guard. This meant I would be spending the whole two weeks in the hospital compound and would not be able to do any of the surveys myself, nor would I be able to monitor the work of those whom I trained. They also said that when we left for Pakistan, we would have to take an escort with us. They did not trust us; therefore, they wanted to control our movements as much as possible. My world shrank, so that my longest daily walk was from my room in the residence area to the hospital.

Boredom

While conducting the workshop, my days were very busy, and I was tired enough at night that my roommate in the ceiling did not bother me. The initial training lasted five days and was attended by doctors from Bamyan, Behsood (located in Wardak Province), Jaghori, Kabul, and Yakawlang (located in Bamyan Province); the education supervisor; and the construction engineer—all coming from Shuhada's various program sites. First, we developed a rapid field assessment tool for the programs, building on an assessment that had already been carried out. Next, local staff members from each of the program areas practiced basic monitoring and evaluation techniques in the classroom. Then they took their surveys to local sites for further practice. For the final survey (see appendix A for a sample), each person would go to an area other than his own to administer the survey, as a way to increase objectivity. In addition, we paired a health person with someone in education when possible. Unfortunately, Aziz, Engineer Muslim, and I could not monitor their efforts in the field, as we were stuck at the hospital.

Finally on the sixth day, the teams left to collect data, a process we thought would take about seven more days—including one day's travel in each direction. When they returned a week later for debriefing and analysis, we spent an additional three days analyzing the health data so that the teams could practice data analysis. The data on schools were quickly hidden from those not involved in the workshops (including other hospital staff). Again, secrecy on this subject was important. We would take that data with us to analyze in Quetta, where we would not have to worry about the Taliban.

The week between the survey development and subsequent data analysis went by very slowly. None of us had work to do and, with limited electricity, computer work was also limited. We had no telephone, Internet, or other means to communicate with the rest of the world. I wrote many pages of detailed notes from the workshops but had little else to write about. The days were a routine of boredom, with a lot of time spent sitting on a hillock within the compound staring out across the valley. I reread the book I had finished in Quetta before coming and also worked through 20 chapters of a Persian grammar book I had brought as a reference guide. You know you are bored when a book on grammar holds your interest. The head of the education sector brought me children's books to read, and my Dari improved. By the time I left, I had mastered the Dari texts for grades one through four. My roommate also seemed to know I was bored and chewed louder at night, though she was still a mystery. By the end of that week, I think I might have welcomed the company had she decided to show herself.

To break the monotony—I was not the only bored person in the group— Aziz, Engineer Muslim, and I walked to a nearby girls' school. We took a roundabout way that avoided the town and the usual footpaths so that the Taliban might not notice our adventure out of the hospital compound. After sitting around for so long, I was puffing by the time we arrived. It was only a 20-minute walk, so I blamed the altitude.

This school was typical of Shuhada's efforts to provide education to the girls of Hazarajat. It was made of stone with a high stone wall around the playground area. The only man on the premises guarded the entry gate. His job was to warn the women and girls inside if any Taliban came to inspect the school, an important job considering that the Taliban had banned education for girls over nine years of age.

At that time, Shuhada paid the girls' teachers a salary. While the salary paid to the girls' teachers was higher than the one the boys' teachers received, the latter also received support from the boys' families in the form of wheat. Our survey results indicated that the different methods of compensation led to two separate problems. First, the girls' teachers were paid their full salary only for the months they were teaching (six or seven months a year), leaving them without an income over the winter months when schools were closed. Thus, in these harsh economic times, the yearly income of the girls' teachers totaled less than that of the uneducated sweepers in the hospital. The boys' teachers, on the other hand, received 40 percent of their salary directly from the boys' families—a monthly amount of wheat for each male student child in the family—and the government paid the remainder of the salary. Unfortunately, crop failures because of the drought made it difficult for families to pay, and they pulled their boys out of school when they could no longer supply the wheat to pay the teacher. In one boys' high school, attendance dropped from 72 to 14 boys in just a few months. The system of payment was a good idea only as long as there was rain and snow to water the crops. In addition, the money for salaries rarely came through from the government, which meant that the boys' teachers also had months without pay. Clearly, there were no easy solutions for compensating both the girls' and the boys' teachers.

Unfortunately, our arrival in Jaghori coincided with the arrival of a letter from Taliban authorities demanding, yet again, that *all* the girl schools be closed immediately. Because of the sensitivity of the problem, we decided not to draw further attention to the schools or to those who worked in them and, therefore, did not survey any of the nearby schools (for boys or girls). Our visit to this particular school went unnoticed but it gave me a sense of what people had to do to maintain their dignity and their sense of control over their own lives. It was not easy for them, and it got worse over the following year. Shuhada staff managed to keep their many schools running in the face of severe poverty, drought, environmental devastation, and oppression by the Taliban—this at a time when the world thought no girls' schools existed.

Food in a Drought

By the end of my first week I felt like I was starving. To compensate, the logistics manager of the hospital brought me fresh home-baked bread every morning. It was the best bread I have ever eaten. These were small round cakes, about two inches thick, that were cooked next to wood coals in a clay oven; the bread was delicious and very filling. The man was delighted to see how I enjoyed them, so much so that he presented me with five fresh loaves for my trip when we left. Yet, bread and tea were not enough to keep me from feeling hungry, though I knew that I was the lucky one in this area where children suffered from chronic malnutrition. For many, bread and tea were all they ate.

A few days after our trip to the school, it was decided that I needed another outing. This time it was because I was clearly losing weight. My companions, gracious hosts as always, were worried about my health and my diet—never mind that I needed to lose a few pounds. As a vegetarian, Afghan food creates some difficulties—including the fact that most of the rice dishes were cooked in meat broth, and hosts always served meat to guests. My companions ate rice and meat daily. Aziz and Engineer Muslim decided that I should go to town and pick out some food for myself—or at least see that there was nothing there to select. Unfortunately, the drought meant that the local market had little to offer in the way of fruits or vegetables. Onions and okra were available, and I was happy to eat that; yet, this created endless problems for my hosts, who loved their meat and meat dishes.

Jaghori was a small market town with a short main street and few buildings that were two stories. We found no vegetables that were worth buying, other than okra and onions. The few eggplants I saw were old and either rotting or drying out. I was shocked on this walk, not by the market, but by the many dry, useless wells we passed. Even the river in the distance was reduced to the point that one could step across it without getting wet.

Shortly after we returned to our rooms, and I was ready to relax when (yet again) Aziz came to tell me that I had a personal visit from one of our talibs. It was the older of the two men who had questioned me previously. This one wanted to talk. He started by saying that "they" (those in charge) knew I was in the Bazaar and that he tried to meet me there. He asked us: "Do you think I am like them? I only work for them because I need to feed my family." Then he told Aziz that it was OK if I wanted to visit people's houses. Aziz saw him as the enemy and told him there were no plans for such visits as we were too busy. Aziz felt it could have been a trick, so he answered on the side of caution.

Yet, this man only wanted to talk, and in fact, he said he wanted psychological counseling. With Aziz translating his Pashto into English for me, we learned that he was a clerk, a bureaucrat, hired by the Taliban to run the office in Jaghori, because he was literate and so many of the others were not. He wanted to talk about himself and his feelings about the 22 years of war. As he talked, he said he was an angry man with lots of rage. He started crying. He wanted instant solutions and medication to take away his depression. He said his life was an accumulation of years of frustration and lack of love. When he talked of how his father treated him, he cried even more. Then he said that when his father would eventually die, he would want to cut his father's body into tiny little pieces, as a sign of his rage. The fact that he cried in front of us was a sign of how devastated he felt. Pashtun men do not cry in public. He also said that he was so angry sometimes that he wanted to kill half the village. Considering his position, he actually had the power to do just that.

As he poured out his frustration and described his life, Aziz found that they carried similar pain, and soon Aziz stopped translating because he was caught up in what the man said. It was as if I was not there. For a brief time, these two men stopped being enemies and became human to each other. They found that they shared the similar trauma of war, family problems, and all the pain of trying to keep the nuclear family together in the face of extended family obligations. When the man left he repeated again that we could go where we wanted without being bothered. What I learned that day should not have been a surprise, but it has stayed with me: not everyone working for the Taliban are talibs. Afghanistan had few places for employment and a very high unemployment rate. This man asked me not to judge him, as he did not agree with all Taliban edicts. Yet, in order to feed his family he had to work for them. He saw his life as having few choices, and those he had were not ones that brought him comfort.

The Women's Clinic

One of the other ways to break the monotony of the days of waiting was to spend time in the hospital and observe the doctors during their three-hour morning outpatient clinic. During this time, approximately 100–150 patients were seen by each of the doctors (male patients by the male doctors, females and children by the woman doctor). There was little time to do more than ask a few questions, take the blood pressure, and prescribe medication. Most women came because of urinary tract infections (UTIs) and pelvic inflammatory disease (PID). One old woman wanted a pill to make her have her periods again, saying that she needed to be able to bear more children so that her husband would not bring another wife into the household. Another wanted to take a pill to be young again because she was afraid that menopause would make her blind. Doctors spent very little time talking to the patients, and patients rarely asked questions. Most patients expected to leave with prescriptions for medication, regardless of their complaints. Most patients felt that the more medicines prescribed the better the doctor.

While I was sitting with the gynecologist, a male doctor came in and asked us to join him. Two children had come in with advanced tuberculosis (TB). The boy, about 12 years of age, had such an extreme case of TB that he had developed a condition called pigeon chest, a condition where the breastbone and rib cage bow outward as a result of lung damage. He also had bone abscesses that came through the skin along his spine. The little girl, his sister, was probably about eight. It was hard to tell children's ages because so many suffered from stunted growth due to chronic malnutrition and micronutrient deficiencies. Her right clavicle was detached from her shoulder and what was left of the bone protruded through the skin.

I had seen bone abscesses and damage from TB on ancient bones in my undergraduate physical anthropology classes, but this was the first time I witnessed them on the living. Apparently the children's family had taken them to a local clinic that specialized in TB but did not take them for the full course of treatment. After a long period of time, the family brought them to this hospital, since, they said, the other "did not work." TB was and is a critical problem worldwide, yet at this time in Afghanistan most hospitals and clinics did not carry the necessary medication to treat it. It was expensive and most clients could not afford to buy it. Internationally run treatment centers were created to provide free medication, but these centers were hard to reach. Many were understaffed and often ran out of needed medication. In addition, those who received treatment often did not complete the full course, leading to drug resistant strains of TB.

Boredom Over

After endless days of waiting, the staff returned with their surveys. All but one group had done an amazing job. Unfortunately, this last one claimed they conducted the surveys but did not write anything down. That pair had spent their time on a side trip to visit the still existing Buddhas of Bamyan. I was not sure if I was angry with them for not doing their job and wasting my time, or because I did not get to go, too. Within a year of this survey the Taliban had destroyed those same Buddhas.

Back in the hospital conference room, we began data analysis utilizing the same participatory process that we applied in the design of the survey. We used the health data to explore various kinds of analysis, procedures, and techniques. In addition, our discussions covered the uses of the data and how to construct a report. The group was enthusiastic and worked long hours, charting their results.

The day we finished the last of the analyses, Aziz and Engineer Muslim decided that we should sneak out of Jaghori before dawn, to avoid further Taliban interference. They did not want the Taliban escorting us or interfering in any way. This decision came in the wake of a dispute in town between a local youth and a talib. We feared the situation could worsen, affecting us. The tension between the local population and their Taliban oppressors was exacerbated by the hardships of the drought and failed food supplies. In addition, local people often tried to resolve old grudges or to manipulate the situation in their favor by giving the Taliban information about their enemies— often these were their neighbors or members of their extended family. Aziz's family was from this region, so he was worried that someone might take revenge on him because of his family's high profile. He had already felt the bite of Taliban imprisonment. It was time to leave.

The Return

That evening we left Jaghori for Quetta. We wanted to slip out of the area without the Taliban being aware of our movement. Late that evening, we drove to a place where we could stop and relax, the home of the hospital administrator. He had come with us to show us the way and to introduce us to his family. In times like these, it was not good for strangers to arrive unannounced.

His home was a massive walled compound, more like a huge adobe fort than a house. Inside the thick outer walls, the house itself was a massive structure with mud brick walls over four feet thick at their base, tapering to just under a foot thick at the ceiling level, which was very high. It seemed like a castle, but because it was dark, I could not get a sense of its total size. The construction was fascinating, with walls so thick that the interior was as cool as a cave. The windowsills in the guest sitting room, where we had our supper, were at least three feet deep, holding flowerpots containing fresh herbs, tomato plants, and various flowers. Our host told us that his family ate fresh vegetables all year. Although I saw electrical lines and light bulbs, we did everything by lantern light. The floor was covered in hand-knotted red rugs, with mats along the walls to sit on and hand embroidered covered bolsters to lean against as we relaxed and enjoyed the conversation with the men of the family.

Shortly after the meal was completed, I was asked if I wanted to go to sleep (more a polite directive than a question). A young woman took me by lantern light to the back of the house, first to the latrine, located outside at the back of the compound, then to an inside washroom to rinse the dust off my hands, face, and feet, and finally to my bedroom. The young woman reassured me that the windowless room was in the interior and was, therefore, very safe. It was small, very cozy, and raised about two feet above the floor level of the hallway. I felt like I had just fallen asleep when I was awakened, at about three in the morning. Within minutes we were continuing our journey toward Quetta.

In Kandahar we were told that I needed an exit visa to leave the country. It was after lunch so we went quickly to the government office and had only a short, nervous wait to see the correct official. If we missed this chance we would have to wait another day, and if we were delayed here, the border would close before we arrived there. It was an anxious time. The Taliban official had the requisite beard and turban, and a large paunch that kept him from getting close to his desk. He was more than happy to stamp my U.S. passport with the required exit stamp—for a small fee of US$100. We both knew it was a bribe. Luckily, I always traveled with one or two hundred-dollar bills hidden in various places on me. I did not even argue. He quietly took the money, placed it in his pocket (it *was* a bribe), stamped my passport, and I was out of there. Aziz, who was waiting by the outer door, was so relieved to see me exit the building that he almost ran toward me to get my attention. We hopped into the car, slammed the doors, and quickly left Kandahar behind us.

The rest of the journey was as uneventful as it was exhausting. We reached the border just before it closed and crossed with no problems. Other than the Pakistani official who wanted a bribe from Engineer Muslim and Aziz, we encountered nothing else to slow us down. There was a comfortable room waiting for me at Lourdes, with a hot shower to remove all the road dust and a real bed under an air conditioner that usually worked. True comfort! I had no complaints.

On the Road to Behsood, Wardak Province

My second trip with Aziz and Engineer Muslim to Hazarajat was so different from the first, yet it was only two months later. I felt I knew them better and I was sure that I was prepared for the adventure. At least I thought I was. This time, over e-mail, I reminded Aziz of the need for the travel permits to the border and basically made a nuisance of myself over details. It helped. Instead of being delayed for three days, we were only delayed for two and a half. Unfortunately, we left Quetta after lunch, making the drive in Afghanistan more difficult as night fell. This time, we had one more passenger, as a Shuhada doctor was returning to his post and wanted to travel with us—there was safety in numbers.

I also came prepared to cope with more boredom and limited food supplies. Unfortunately, it was no longer mango season so food was an issue. I made sure my scarves were large and black, my dresses longer and looser. I packed several books, a jar of peanut butter, and some packets of noodle soup. We took fresh bread with us, as well as dried apricots and almonds. And this trip was planned so that we would drive from Quetta to Wardak, spend five days there, and return by way of Kabul and Jalalabad, crossing the Torkham border into Pakistan, to arrive at Peshawar. What could go wrong?

As before, we needed guards and two taxis to the border, which we crossed at about 3:00 PM. This time we had one taxi to take us all the way to Kandahar. We arrived in this city just as the sun was setting, 7:00 PM. As we entered the city, we were stopped by some Taliban youth, members of the V&V—the Vice and Virtue, who always reminded me of teen gang members. They stood

Hazarajat, in central Afghanistan. Photo taken in 2000 on the road to Behsood.

Farmer threshing wheat in Hazarajat. Photo taken in 2000.

around the check post, acting tough and harassing anyone they could—the age or gender of the person did not stop them. Aziz got in an argument with one because he was demanding that I, the only female in the car, sit in the cramped, back of the station wagon, behind the backseats. Aziz told him he should not expect foreign women to act as local women. He also told the young man to remember his culture—that Pashtuns honor guests and I was a guest in their country. Usually the "guest card" was all that would be needed to remind someone of his cultural obligation toward strangers. There is a saying in Pashto: "Guests are a gift from Allah. To take good care of a guest brings honor to one's family and blessings from God; to treat a guest badly would mean dishonor and shame." This young man was not moved by the argument and tried to use threats. Aziz stayed calm and showed how the back of the taxi was filled with our equipment and the backseat was filled with men. There was nowhere else for me to sit. In the end the talib let us go, and I got to stay in my front seat.

Actually, although it took an argument to keep me there, the seat was not that comfortable. I tried over and over to relax, but the seat was lumpy and seemed to be filled with small blocks of some kind. It turns out that the driver hid his cassette tapes in the passenger seat. The Taliban forbade music and they loved to destroy any cassette they found. As one traveled the country, it was common to see trees and posts wrapped with the tapes from countless destroyed cassettes. The driver told me that the Taliban were less likely to search the seat of the passenger, and the forbidden tapes could be easily accessed when driving between towns. This driver loved his music and was clearly no friend of the Taliban.

By the time we reached Kandahar, it was closing down for the night, and there was no chance for another taxi. Engineer Muslim tried to convince our driver to take us all the way to Wardak. As he was Hazara, he said he was willing to go as far as Ghazni, where his family lived. I was nervous about driving onward, and I was tired and hungry. I also needed to find a toilet and a chance to stretch my legs. Luckily on this trip I had the name of a contact in Kandahar, an Afghan friend's uncle who worked for a UN agency. In fact, this man's son had stayed in my house in Islamabad while he studied for his exams. Engineer Naqib was expecting us but worried when we arrived so late. Over the last several months, Taliban influence and control in rural areas was weakening, and he was worried for our safety. He cautioned us to get a hotel and stay the night in Kandahar. "The countryside was no longer safe for travel," he said. "The situation has radically changed over the last two months." Because we would be spending more time on the main Kandahar–Kabul road, there would be a greater risk of being caught by bandits. He could tell that Engineer Muslim was not translating their conversation so he took me aside and tried his best to persuade me to stay.

Engineer Muslim had made up his mind: we would continue our journey. Both Aziz and I were angry, but without another word on the subject, we left the UN compound and headed out of town toward Kabul. It was already dark. We had only used the toilet at the UN office, not even staying long enough to eat supper. Although it seemed crazy to have gone on in the face of such warnings, it would have been difficult to stay in the city. The Taliban monitored hotels, so we could not have stayed in one. Nor could we have stayed in an Afghan home (foreigners were banned from those). We could not have stayed in an NGO or UN guesthouse, as we had not made prior arrangements or gotten proper clearances. We really did have to travel onward. But I was angry with Engineer Muslim, as head of logistics, for not planning for this problem. We left too late in the day from Quetta to arrive anywhere near our destination, putting us at greater risk. Unlike the last trip, that took us to the western edge of Hazarajat, this one would take us almost to Kabul, before turning off the main road into the highland area of Wardak Province. The drive from Kandahar to Kabul at that time took about 18 hours. We could expect to be on the road for over 24 hours, a long exhausting drive. As we bounced along in the dark, I worried. I felt very strongly that we should have stayed in Kandahar. The drive was made worse by my sulking.

As we drove, the beating I received from the car, as I was bounced and tossed around, exhausted me even further. I was amazed, yet again, that, though taxi drivers started out by being careful of potholes, bomb craters, and other road hazards, they soon became almost maniacal. It was not long before this man was driving over all but the deepest craters as he tried to keep his speed up to at least 30 kph. We were thrown around so much that it was impossible to get comfortable. Yet it had been a long day, and I finally bounced my way into an exhausted sleep.

I don't know how long I slept, but the car stopping at a roadside restaurant woke me. It was after 10:00 PM and our driver was tired. He stopped here for a break and found out that it was unsafe to continue any further until morning. There were many cars and trucks pulled into a rough circle, much like cowboys circling the wagons in an old western movie. The trucks formed the outer ring and the smaller cars were scattered inside the circle. As on our last trip, I was to sleep in the car. This time the back was made into a bed and I was left alone. It was so dark that I could not tell where the men were. Every half hour I was awakened by men with flashlights acting as security for the area—they would wander by and shine their flashlight into the cab. It was a very long night and I started to miss the road.

At about 3:00 AM I got my wish. We left the car park and resumed our journey toward Wardak, joined by a slow trickle of other cars. I slept much of the next leg of the trip, with Engineer Muslim waking me each time my *chador* slipped from my head. Sometime in the mid-morning we reached Ghazni. Our driver was exhausted, as were we. We looked for the taxi that would take us the rest of the way. Engineer Muslim, Aziz, and I bundled into a Russian car that looked to be at least 50 years old. It had hard wooden seats and a very weak engine. About half-way up the rugged mountain road to Behsood (our destination, located in Wardak Province), we had to look for another taxi. This poor car just could not make it. At a small village along the road, we finally found another taxi, and we completed the drive in an old beat-up Toyota.

We puffed into the hospital grounds at Behsood in the early afternoon. As before, the staff were waiting for us and anxious to start. And as before, we were bunking at the hospital, a small outpost that was clean and comfortable. Of course, anything was comfortable after that drive. The hospital was a small one-story L-shaped building with a dry latrine behind the building near the outer wall. Near my room in the hospital building was a washing room, a square room with a depressed area that took up about half the floor space. This was the area where one stood to bathe. A wood stove with a built-in water tank heated the water and the room. When I was ready to bathe, one of the hospital cleaners would put two buckets of cold water in the room so that I could mix the hot and cold water to the right temperature for a bucket bath. It was a daily pleasure as the steamy room gave me a chance to warm up and relax. It was September, and the season was turning from summer to fall at this high altitude, with warm days and cold nights, so I looked forward to the warmth of the bathing room.

Unfortunately, in the exuberance of welcoming us to Behsood, the local staff had planned a meal out with the local community head, at his home. And, because they remembered I did not eat meat, they had arranged for me to have fried fish from the market. I was the only person to eat the fish and I was the only person to become very ill within hours of the meal. In fact, well before our first afternoon's workshop was adjourned, I was losing my lunch and everything else over the side of the patio into the flower bed. But, if one has to be sick in a country like Afghanistan, staying at a hospital where I was giving doctors training was useful. I had five doctors and many nurses trying to help me recover. And, the program did not halt while I was sick. Aziz took over the introduction and presentation of the findings from the survey and the strategic planning meeting that had been held in August in Quetta. I was able to get better, and by the next morning I was helping the group of doctors plan ways to implement their strategic plan.

Health Care and Community Mobilization

The roads between villages in this highland area were so bad that a four-wheel-drive pickup could only go about 10 kph (5 mph). Cows seemed to pass us as we drove to visit the district hospitals. Here, the presence of the Taliban was minimal and we were free to explore the area. Shuhada had established four hospitals in this region, providing minimum acute care and emergency surgery. On this trip, our plan was to set up a community health outreach and monitoring system for the hospitals and their trained birth attendants. Communities were very isolated from each other, making planning interesting.

This area was less affected by the drought than Jaghori. Locals planted two kinds of wheat—winter wheat that was sown on uncultivated hillsides in the fall and harvested in spring after the rains and snow were gone; the other wheat was planted in cultivated areas near water sources. This year only the latter grew. The other wheat crops failed from lack of rain and snow. Luckily, the river was still high enough that people could use the water for irrigation, keeping starvation away. On this trip I saw fewer cases of malnutrition and less stunting. I was told that the following year would be risky as there would be fewer seeds to plant. Because of lower crop yields, many families were eating the portion of wheat they would normally leave for seeding next year's crops.

Due to the dispersed settlement pattern in this region, trained community health workers were a vital link between households and the local hospital. Distances were great and roads often impassible. Getting health care information out to the communities was important for reducing common illnesses like diarrheal diseases or respiratory infections. While we were running the workshop, a man walked into the hospital with a knife wound in the stomach. He had come with friends by donkey from quite a distance. The surgeon repaired him and he lost some bowel but that was all—other than the peritonitis, of course. Such incidents, like knife or gunshot wounds, were common. In our survey (see appendix A for a sample of the survey) we found that this was widespread, and people were willing to travel great distances for health care at Shuhada facilities, often bypassing services that might have been closer. For example, one man came to Jaghori Hospital from Shahristan, a two-day journey by car. In another area, a woman was brought to the Yakawlang hospital on a three-day journey by donkey.

In many ways, developing community health outreach served as a political device to nurture civil society structures that had been destroyed by war, rivalry, and out-migration. This part of Afghanistan was extremely poor, but the people were willing to move toward (or back to) unified systems that could benefit all. The team had to educate me as I worked with them to facilitate a plan of action that they would be able to implement. I learned that vil-

Mosque and community center in Wardak. Photo taken in 2000.

Shuhada staff working on a community health plan in Wardak. Photo taken in 2000.

lages were little more than extended family compounds and that mosques were centrally located and shared by many such households; mosques often had meeting areas that could be used to encourage community programs and processes. We worked in the mornings on our plans and spent most afternoons walking from one community to another, interviewing health workers and community leaders, in order to understand the best way to proceed. Unlike the Jaghori trip where I was restricted to the hospital grounds, here I was able to get a feel for the place and the people. We worked hard on the program because the doctors were needed back in their own areas: Yakawlang, Jaghori, and Kabul. The five days passed very quickly.

The Road to Kabul

On the sixth morning, we awakened in the predawn hours. The frost had already blackened the last of the zinnias in the garden. It was time to head back to Pakistan. The medical director, a man with a lot of charisma and an easy laugh, offered to drive us to Kabul so that we could get a taxi that would take us to the Torkham border, on the way to Peshawar. From there I would be able to call my friends in Islamabad so that they could come get me. It was the fastest way home for me, though it meant that Engineer Muslim and Aziz would have to find transport from Peshawar to Quetta. They seemed more willing to go the Pakistan route by bus than travel back along the Taliban-controlled Kabul–Kan-

Dramatic scenery
of rugged cliffs
and barren hills
north of Kabul.

dahar road. For one thing, the roads in Pakistan were super highways compared to those in Afghanistan, and there were no Taliban check posts to deal with at that time in Pakistan. They would only have to fend off demands for bribes.

The trip to Kabul took only a few hours; it was a much easier drive downhill in this four-wheel-drive pickup than it was going uphill in a broken down taxi. As we approached Kabul, I saw an area I had not seen before. It was completely bombed out, with only the skeletons of buildings standing. And it went on for miles like this. Then we drove through some areas that were less destroyed but terribly run-down. Finally, we reached the taxi stand, where we could get the Jalalabad–Torkham taxi.

As I waited for the men to negotiate our ride, a beggar, a woman in a blue chadari, came knocking at my window. I had one five-Afghani note left, so I slipped it out the window to her. It was worth less than a penny but other women saw what I had done, and within seconds, my car was surrounded. The women were pounding on the windows, rattling the doors, and trying to persuade me to give to them money. I was shocked and a little scared. These women were desperate and hungry, and I obviously looked like I could help, but I did not have any more money. The men rushed back to the taxi and formed a phalanx around me so that I could get to our new taxi. They chided me for giving money and drawing attention to myself in such a way. They wanted to get all of us out of Kabul before the Taliban knew we were there. My attempt at kindness almost back-fired.

Reflections

In spite of all the valiant efforts to keep the girls' schools open, Shuhada was falling behind. The Taliban were trying hard to close all girls' schools, but what they could not accomplish through intimidation and oppression, the drought and resulting starvation would. People had very little money to send their children—boys or girls—to school as the drought continued into its fifth year. In this rural area, Shuhada had an ingenious method of paying the teachers in a cashless, subsistence economy. It also promoted community participation and was, minus the drought, sustainable. But by the time I visited the region, families did not have wheat to spare. I doubted there would be seeds left for next year's planting. And the following year was, indeed, worse. The rains did not come until the winter of 2001. I was overwhelmed seeing their struggle merely to survive. Yet, some schools were open and health service delivery continued, even in very remote areas. It was a heroic effort by many dedicated people.

The travel situation and decisions in Afghanistan for Shuhada caused me great worry and distress, but I found out later that there was much I did not know. On the first trip, Engineer Muslim said that, for my protection, we would not stay at a rest house along the highway. We drove through the night and encountered car trouble that left us all very vulnerable. That attempt to keep me safe placed us in another kind of danger. On the second trip, we were warned that the Taliban had lost control of the rural areas between Kandahar and Kabul to local factions, and I felt we needed to stay in Kandahar over night. Again, Engineer Muslim decided to forge ahead. My contact at the UN had even taken me aside, hoping that if I knew the situation, I would pressure my companions to stay in town for the night. Generally, the international person has the greatest say in decision making, and he hoped I would use that to override Engineer Muslim's decision. I tried, as did Aziz, but Engineer Muslim was adamant.

All this sounds like we were taking the advice of someone who was making very poor decisions. What I learned several years later was that we could not have stayed in Kandahar because we would have faced an even greater threat if we had been found by the Taliban; Engineer Muslim was on the their "most wanted" list, and had they caught him and us, they would have killed him and most probably put Aziz and the taxi driver in jail (again). Aziz had been in jail more than once and had been tortured each time. Engineer Muslim was a former general when Afghanistan was ruled by a pro-Soviet government and was thus high on the Taliban's most wanted list. Even so, they were not after him, but he had been caught in a wicked twist of fate. In fact, the Taliban wanted to find and kill another man with the same name, but if they had stopped and questioned Engineer Muslim, they would not have taken the time to clarify his identity or given him a trial to see if they had the right man. After the Taliban gained control of Kabul they began to search for those whom they saw as their enemies, including a man known as Engineer Muslim, from Kabul. The man with whom I traveled was from central Bamyan, where he was living with his very large family. It was winter when our Engineer Muslim received word that the Taliban were coming to kill him and his family, even though he was not the man for whom they searched. He escaped at the last minute with his entire family, walking over the snowy mountain passes from Hazarajat, all the way to Quetta. All the while I thought they were keeping the Taliban from knowing about me, but they were really protecting Engineer Muslim.

Engineer Muslim never told me this story; I learned it later from Aziz. Had I known, I would have been a more willing traveler. Instead, I had been angry at Engineer Muslim, feeling that he had placed us in what I thought was greater danger. The Afghan way of protecting friends and others from bad news through silence creates frustration for those of us who are used to being participants in finding solutions to those problems.

I think what I carried away from this experience was a deeper understanding of life under a fascist and racist regime. From these trips to Hazarajat I felt like I gained an understanding of life in Nazi Germany. I often stopped to wonder if this was what it was like for people living under Hitler. In the struggle to survive, some people would take advantage of others, only to fall victim to the same process later. It was easy to see how a person's honor and freedom could be eroded as he tried to keep his family alive. As we drove through Hazarajat, a mountainous area full of caves, it was common for the driver or Aziz or someone else to point to caves where the locals knew the Taliban had thrown the bodies of people whom they had killed. Weeks before the Taliban left Hazarajat in 2001, they rounded up over 300 men in

Aziz (far left) and the author (foreground on the right) with others looking for sites to build schools in Faryab Province in 2005.

Yakawlang (located in the northwestern part of Bamyan Province) and shot them. One of those men had been an educator who had participated in the Shuhada strategic planning workshop. On this trip, even more than the one to Kabul in 1998, I was deeply moved because I saw the way a group of people were oppressed solely because of their ethnicity and their religious affiliation.

This place touched my heart, as I know it had touched so many others who worked with these very resilient and determined people. I gained a better understanding of the plight of a minority group, and a better understanding of the Taliban. At the same time that the population struggled to survive under a repressive and very brutal regime, they faced one of the worst droughts in history. So many of the children were older than they looked because of stunting caused by chronic malnutrition. And they aged very quickly, once mature. The "old" woman who cleaned my room at the hospital was actually in her forties, but you could not tell by looking at her; I thought she was in her late sixties or seventies.

My next trip to this region came under happier times—post-Taliban and post-9/11. I helped Aziz, and others, bring schools and teacher training to Hazarajat. As Country Representative for AFSC (the Quakers) from 2004 to 2007, I visited and helped to ensure that hundreds of girls and boys would attend school in Bamyan, Faryab, Balkh, and Kabul. Aziz was the deputy director and head of finance for their Kabul office. Together, we set up programs for teacher training, psychosocial wellness, and child-to-child activities; we even established some science labs. I never saw the Buddha statues of Bamyan, but I have seen the smiling faces of girls and boys attending school.

Chapter 3

Herat

𝒥t was the summer of 2001, and I had been planning the trip from Peshawar, Pakistan, to Herat, Afghanistan, for several weeks. It took even more weeks to actually get there. It never became easy to go inside Afghanistan to areas controlled by the Taliban. Every time I applied for a visa from the Afghan Consulate in Peshawar the rules changed. The previous year, I had begun working as a technical advisor for an Afghan NGO, Coordination of Humanitarian Assistance (CHA). This organization had helped me get my visa for the work I did with Shuhada. At that time, the man who had this job because he had personal contacts in the Afghan Consulate got me a visa within an hour of presenting my passport. But, in 2001, the same man had to apply "properly" and be patient, as the visa came through Kabul's Foreign Ministry; he was told that it could take weeks. It did. So I waited.

At this time, CHA had programs in at least five Afghan provinces and employed over 700 full-time staff. I was the only expat on their payroll at that time and worked with them for two years. They used a holistic approach to development and relief aid, working simultaneously on infrastructure, agriculture, education, and health. In addition, they had computer- and English-language-training centers in Herat and Peshawar. One of the hallmarks of CHA was their ability to integrate women into all areas of their programs and into all strata of management. They were the only NGO with a woman in charge of logistics and another as head of human resources. It was their stated goal to have women in every department. No international NGO was as effective as CHA in gender mainstreaming.

The director of CHA hired me to develop a mental health program that would help their staff cope with the hardships of work in Afghanistan under the Taliban and with the stress of living as refugees in Pakistan. Several managers told me of abuses by the Taliban when they were trying to run relief programs in Afghanistan. For example, one told me of the time the Taliban arrested him because he did not have a proper, untrimmed beard. They locked him, along with other men, in a shipping container for almost a week as punishment. The container was in the hot sun and the men had to share a limited water supply. Everyone told me that they could not feel safe in their own country, but in Pakistan, as refugees, they faced other hardships, including police harassment and resentment from the local population. One of the risks Afghan staff faced in Peshawar was being picked up by Pakistani police and handed over to the Taliban at the Torkham border near Peshawar. There were many stories in the office of staff who suffered from nightmares and who thought they were more angry and violent because of their experiences. The head of CHA knew that he and his staff needed help and asked me to find a way to do this.

CHA, as part of their strategic plan, also wanted to develop mental health programs for their clinics in western Afghanistan. Before I could do this I needed to have a better understanding of the problems faced by those who lived inside. There were reports from Afghanistan of huge mental health problems and PTSD (posttraumatic stress disorder), because of the horrific human rights abuses that had become almost normalized during the war against the Soviets and the subsequent interethnic fighting. Under the Taliban, things were deteriorating even more. One story circulated that summed up the frustrations families faced and the violence that ensued:

> A man leaves his home to shop at the local market and encounters an angry *talib*, who beats him. Frustrated and angry, the man returns home and takes his anger out on his wife by beating her. She turns around and beats her kids. The children get mad because they were unfairly beaten and kick the family dog. The dog runs out of the compound and into the street, where it bites a *talib*. The *talib* is angry and hits the first man he sees. . . . (MSF 1999)

It was clear from all the stories I heard that there was a need to address psychosocial issues. In Herat, several agencies, including the International Assistance Mission (IAM) and Médicins Sans Frontières (MSF),[7] were working on mental health through clinical perspectives. In addition, IAM had conducted counseling for groups of women in community settings. The program at CHA would be the first to address the psychosocial wellness of their own staff and within their programs. And CHA was looking to use a wellness/preventive model.

My Team

The purpose of this trip to Herat was to conduct a brief survey of mental health and psychosocial wellness of the Herat-based CHA staff and their program beneficiaries (see appendix A for a sample of the survey). In order to develop the program on psychosocial wellness I was to mentor and train a brother–sister team, Tawab and Naderah, who would eventually take over and run the program. It was my job to develop the program and provide the initial training/capacity building for the staff. This program would be housed within but not restricted to CHA's health sector—it was hoped that it would also eventually be connected to the education and development sectors, as well. Because we were working to break new ground and trying to develop a program that would be simple to replicate and based in Afghan culture and traditions, we first needed to have background data.

Initially, I gave Naderah and Tawab some basic training in survey and interviewing techniques. We also explored the field of community-based psychosocial wellness, as it applied to development. A friend, Nina Joy Lawrence, a licensed counselor, trained us all in Focusing. Focusing is used worldwide by therapists and others in health and mental health settings, as well as in community programs (Focusing Institute 2003). We worked to adapt it to Afghan culture, using metaphors and methods with which Afghans would feel comfortable. For example, Afghans are not comfortable sharing inner thoughts; thus, Focusing is valuable because, unlike many other therapeutic methods, it does not rely on self-disclosure to promote healing.

Naderah had worked at CHA as the program supervisor in the agency's English-language and computer school in Peshawar, where she had started as an English teacher. She and her brother came to Peshawar with their family as refugees in the late 1980s. This new position gave her brother, who was unemployed, as were many educated Afghan refugees in Pakistan, a chance to work. Tawab would interview men in this project, but he was also critically needed as Naderah's escort or mahram. Without him at her side, she would not be allowed do her job.

Because it was assumed that I would get a visa quickly, Naderah and Tawab traveled ahead of me to Herat to start interviewing office staff and community members. We were not sure when I might be able to join them, but because they went overland on an exhausting three days' journey that took them first to Kabul, then to Kandahar, and finally north to Herat, we were sure they would not have to wait long.

They went by office car from Peshawar to Torkham (the border crossing near the Khyber Pass between Pakistan and Afghanistan that linked Peshawar and Kabul), where they crossed the border by foot and took public transport to Kabul. That drive took them from the hot lowland areas around Jalalabad up a steep twisty mountain road to Kabul. There they spent a few days with their family before continuing on to Herat. The drive itself was arduous—lots of rugged mountains and no real roads. Dust billowed around the cars and buses as they sped along at 10–15 mph, turning a 100-mile trip into an all-day journey.

Naderah told me that this was a long, difficult journey, and that it felt even longer because she had to wear the sweltering chadari. It was made of a synthetic fabric that draped from an embroidered cap. She looked out on the world through an embroidered grillwork that prevented peripheral vision and disguised her identity. It also prevented the movement of air because it was ankle length. She had to keep it in place at all times. Imagine riding in the sweltering heat (over 100°F) in a synthetic tent, sitting in a crowded bus with no shock absorbers, traveling over very bumpy roads.

For my trip, I wore a long, grey, cotton buttoned, floor-length coat (*hijab*), with a scarf to cover all my hair. It covered me from head to toe and kept the Taliban from bothering me. Underneath I wore my usual Pakistani shalwar kamees. Naderah, like most young Afghan women, wore the ubiquitous chadari over her long sleeved blouse, long skirt, and white pants. While it took me five minutes or more to be ready to go out in my coat and scarf, it took her only a few seconds to don the all-covering chadari. In public, I had the advantage. Because of the loss of peripheral vision and the ability to see down, Naderah easily tripped over holes in the sidewalk. The chadari might be easy to wear, but it was stifling hot and made negotiating one's way around broken sidewalks and streets hazardous.

During the bus ride to Herat, Naderah, an outspoken woman of 30, said the worst part was having to rely on her brother to talk for her when any officials had questions. She could only sit on the bus covered in her chadari, trying to remain inconspicuous. If the Taliban learned that she worked for an NGO, she and her brother could be beaten and jailed. On this trip, they carried no office information with them, as protection against possible searches. Luckily, they arrived in Herat without problems and stayed at the home of the brother of another colleague. His house was on the outskirts of town, away from street noises and Taliban searches.

Herat by an ICRC Flight

For security reasons, CHA insisted that I travel to Herat by air. It was never easy to fly to Afghanistan, and this trip was no exception. At that time ICRC provided a valuable service to foreign aid workers, and they had flights throughout Afghanistan almost every day, going to Herat twice a week, but seats were limited. Non-ICRC staff were allocated seats on a first come, first serve basis. But, even having a seat did not guarantee you would be on the flight. They could bump you off if an ICRC official decided to travel at the last moment. Unfortunately for me, when I had no visa I had a seat on the plane, but when I got the visa there was no seat. It took almost two weeks of waiting before I was finally able to leave for Herat.

On the morning of my flight, I arrived at the ICRC office in University Town, Peshawar. There, as with other flights into Afghanistan, the agency took charge and checked my baggage and documents. I now felt like an old hand at this. The plane, a small one that carried 14 passengers, with cargo in the back, left Peshawar at 9:30 AM and stopped in Jalalabad and Kabul before arriving in Herat (by noon). From there it would return to Peshawar.

At each stop someone got off and others joined us, but the plane never filled completely. Those who got on in Kabul were, for the most part, heading back to Peshawar. They had me worried as they told of the strict search of all luggage by Taliban authorities and I remembered that I carried pictures of people with me—I had forgotten to take them out when I changed purses for traveling. The Taliban forbade photos of people. I had my favorite picture of my son hugging his girlfriend. I could only worry and wonder what the Taliban would say when they saw it. Carrying such pictures could get me in trouble with the Taliban and get me banned from traveling on future ICRC flights, if they made a fuss. At this point, I went through the mental checklist: cover my hair (check); wear nonwhite pants under my dresses (check); and wear socks in the 100 degree heat (yikes! No socks!). Where were my socks anyway? Packed away with the other winter clothing in the back of my closet, of course. By the time the plane landed in Herat I was nervous, imagining all the things that could go wrong. Since I had been through Kabul many times, I knew what the grilling could be like. There was nothing I could do but get off the plane and hope for the best. Worry would not help.

As I stepped off the stairs of the plane, I was surprised. The airport seemed relaxed. So relaxed, in fact, that I failed to get the entrance stamp in my passport. I completely forgot as I was being rushed toward the ICRC car that was waiting to drive me to their office in town. Luckily, the government official whose job was to stamp the passports with entry and exit visas rode with me. He quickly realized that I was the newcomer. He and the others in the car laughed as he told me to send my passport back to the airport on Saturday (this was Tuesday) and he would be happy to stamp it for me. He laughed and said: "Don't worry, it happens all the time." This official was so relaxed about things that the day we were to leave, he didn't come to the airport and we all left without exits stamps. No one cared.

By the time I arrived, Naderah and Tawab were ready to return to their home and family in Peshawar. They were tired of the Taliban. They were booked on Ariana Airlines for Kabul the following day.

The City

I landed at Herat's airport at the beginning of a summer thunderstorm but ready to learn what I could. In 2001, Herat (located in the province of the same name) was the second largest city in Afghanistan (350,000) with almost 200,000 IDPs (internally displaced persons).[8] It was an ancient city located in the west of the country, near Iran—often seen as the sister city to Iran's Mashad. In the center of this economic hub sat the fort that contained the remnants of the citadel built by Alexander the Great and turned into a fort by Timurid rulers.[9] The beautiful Friday Mosque (originally built in AD 1200)[10] formed the hub of the city. The Heratis had been one of the first to resist Soviet influences and to refuse communist rule. It was here that some of the first aerial bombings by the Soviet and Afghan armies occurred in the late 1970s. During this war much of Herat was destroyed. In the lull between that war and the coming of the Taliban, Herat was quickly rebuilt under the leadership of their traditional head, Ismail Khan—a warlord. In 1996, when the Taliban advanced to the city, the Heratis pragmatically decided to surrender rather than have their city destroyed again by fighting.

Heratis viewed themselves as urban and cultured, asserting their history, steeped in the arts, poetry, and music. The Taliban, in contrast, were mostly tribal villagers from the border area of Afghanistan and Pakistan. The Heratis saw the Taliban as country bumpkins, who were violent, uncouth, and ignorant of the arts, proper living, and social refinement. Although Herat was predominantly Sunni, its close economic ties to Shia Iran made the Taliban suspicious. In addition, many Heratis had waited out the Afghan–Soviet war in Iran, with whom they were historically close. Although most Heratis felt ambivalent toward Iran, because of the way they were treated as refugees, they hated the Taliban.

By the time I arrived in Herat in the summer of 2001, pressure from the West to try to force the Taliban to relax their edicts and change their policy toward women and children only increased their mistrust of foreigners. Because of this, expats could stay only in officially sanctioned guesthouses within the city, such as the UN guesthouse. There were so few available spaces that aid workers often shared rooms. In addition, we were bound by so many rules that work and travel were very difficult. For example, Afghan women could travel by air only if they used Afghan public transportation, such as by Ariana Afghan Airlines, or by road using public transportation, as Naderah had done, and never in NGO or UN vehicles. All my interviews clearly revealed that everyone was fed up with the Taliban. There were scores of harsh rules, but even worse was the fact that one could be caught and punished for some new, undeclared edict.

It was a very dangerous time. One day, the young CHA driver gave me a quick tour of the city. He told me how it felt for him under the rule of the Taliban. He was angry and felt helpless in his anger, as there was no way to deal with grievances when he was abused by a talib. He also wanted to show me the central park where the Taliban hung their enemies by their feet until they died, and then left the bodies there for days as a warning to others. As we neared the place, I was afraid to look. I knew there were two men who had recently been sentenced to this punishment, but I could not look to see if they were there—what I might see was too painful.

The continuing drought created huge problems as villagers from the countryside poured into the city looking for food and work as their crops failed. A series of IDP camps were established within an hour's drive of the city. Taliban officials were reluctant to allow aid workers access to these IDPs and frequently diverted or prevented food and other aid meant for these hungry, poor people from reaching them.

The People

In Afghan homes, people tried to leave politics and the Taliban behind. Yet, even there, Taliban edicts intruded. Television, movies, and music were banned. Weddings, once a time for dancing and music, no longer sparkled with the sounds of keyboards, drums, and stringed instruments. People would hide in the back of their houses, trying to enjoy themselves, fearful that members of the V&V might hear.

As in most other areas of Afghanistan, a single room could be used for many purposes—family gatherings, guests, dining, and sleeping. The mats used for sitting during the day were covered with clean sheets and transformed into beds at night. My first night in Herat was spent with the family of the head of the health sector. After a wonderful meal I fell asleep where I had been sitting. As I slept the women cleared the room around me and placed a mosquito net over my "bed."

The mosquito net did more than keep out mosquitoes. In Herat, Leishmaniasis is widespread. The local term is *soldona*. It is a parasite that is transmitted by the sand fly, a small biting fly. The local name refers to the time it takes the bite wound to heal—one year. When the sand fly takes a blood meal, it injects the parasite into the skin, where it develops a large circular sore. Over the course of the year this sore spreads and forms a crust with an angry red ring around it. When healed, Leishmaniasis leaves a telltale, pitted crater of darker skin. The only positive aspect is that once someone has been bitten, the person has immunity against more infections. In Herat almost everyone has a scar, usually on the cheek or nose.

Education

The Taliban announced on the radio that people were not to have home schools. Anyone caught sending their children to or running a home school would be punished. This created enormous stress on parents and teachers, but the threats did not stop Herati families from trying to educate their children. When the V&V raided a home looking for evidence of schoolbooks, radios, TVs, and VCRs, the children knew to hide their books and pencils. Even the youngest students knew it was important to keep the secret.

I visited several underground schools and found it both encouraging and heart wrenching. The first one was in the heart of the city, at the home of one of the teachers. The principal struggled to keep the school hidden from the authorities, as children streamed in and out of the building each day. The house was a simple place in need of repair, but it was filled to capacity. Classes were held on the porch and in a dim room that needed lights but had none. There was barely enough room to keep the children out of the hot sun. The kids, both young boys and girls, told me how dangerous it was for them each day as they walked to and from school. One small girl told us that she was followed one day by a talib, who she feared would have beaten her if he caught her. If she led him to the school, everyone would have been beaten and her school would have been closed. She started to go down one alley after another in the congested area near the school. Finally, she lost him in the crowd, but she went home instead of continuing on to school because she was so frightened.

A boys' school in a village north of Herat in 2003.

We did a small write and draw activity with the children of this school. I distributed crayons and paper and asked each of them to draw a picture of their lives. Although I did not prompt them, most drew pictures of themselves facing a talib who carried a whip or a gun. They were clearly afraid of the Taliban and some told me of a time when they had been beaten or whipped. The pictures were starkly done in reds and blacks, even though other colors were available, indicative of the levels of violence and the depth of insecurity the children felt.

Where the first school was poor, the second school was well off, owned by a teacher who had more resources. It was on several acres of land at the outskirts of Herat, with the house/school in the center. A high wall surrounded the property, which was filled with fruit trees, flowers, and more. We drove through the gate, parked the car, and walked down a long path covered by grape vines filled with fruit almost ready to pick. The location was so beautiful, green, and healthy—such a contrast to the destruction common in other areas. I longed to stay.

There were two women teachers, each holding two shifts of classes a day; each shift had about 40 students per class (for a total of 160 students in four classes a day). Like the city school, both boys and girls attended, though the classes themselves were segregated. When we arrived, the kids were sitting in two groups on tarps on the porch. They were clean and seemed motivated to learn. When the teachers took us inside to talk over tea, the youngsters sat on the porch and listened. I was surprised that they did not start talking amongst themselves. They just sat very quietly, though some strained to get a look at me through the screen on the window. I was not given the chance to meet the students, as I had in the city school. The teachers wanted to spend their time with me instead.

Later, I visited a poor school in the central area. Even though it was called a *madrasa* (religious school), the Taliban did not approve of its policies or curriculum. Instruction included more than memorization of the Quran: children learned literacy and numeracy, and the textbooks were based on themes of peace and conflict resolution. Teachers said the children were all glad to be there and studied hard. The day before our visit one boy was followed by a talib, so he went a roundabout way to get back to his own house. This happened often. The children told me that they worried about school and that they saw their parents worry about economic and political problems. All were afraid of the Taliban. Again, I handed out paper and crayons to the children. Two girls drew the Taliban with sticks that they use to beat the people. The children told me how they felt about the events in their lives. They told me that their parents were worried about the fighting that was close to Herat (there was fighting between Taliban and other groups in the neighboring province) and about the drought.

Back at the CHA office, I spoke with Tariq, a man of 47 years. He told me that, since the average life span for Afghans was 44, he was doing well. Tariq told me that he wanted to show me his life and tell me about his family. He had five daughters and three sons. The daughters should have been in school and some would have been in college now if life had been different; he related this with great sadness in his voice. He said he had no tears left. Then he showed me his prized possessions—his paintings. Tariq was an accomplished miniaturist in the Herati style. This is a style of painting that depicts scenes, like sitting in a house reading a book, in intricate detail, evoking poetic imagery through stylized positioning and details of people and objects. This passion for art was what kept him going in the face of all the destruction and trauma from the wars and from Taliban. He knew that the existence of these pieces, if found, would get him beaten and possibly jailed and the art destroyed. But, he confided, it was the art that kept him alive. He painted, and that brought him some calmness. I knew he had taken a great risk to bring his artwork to the office to show me. Had he been stopped on the way, a common practice by the Taliban and the V&V, he would have been severely punished.

Community Health

On our first and only day together, Naderah and I (with Tawab as our escort) went to talk to the doctors and counselors at the IAM, followed by a visit to a clinic run by MSF. IAM had developed the first clinical program on mental health in Afghanistan. Their work was clinic based, with community outreach by their community health workers. It focused on mental illnesses and depression. MSF also worked through clinics and had completed an extensive survey on depression in Herat. They documented the effects of Taliban restrictions on the urban population, showing the damage to the mental health and well-being of women caused by the restrictive edicts (MSF 1999).

In the afternoon, we visited World Food Programme (WFP) projects at an IDP camp, including a pasta-making program where women in the camp

Surveyors collecting data for UNIFEM on women and families in a village north of Herat, 2003.

earned money making pasta out of high-protein flour, which was then distributed in the camps, and a child nutrition and feeding program. The MSF doctor had told us the feeding program actually added to his work because they did not use proper food preparation standards and many children become sick eating their food. Malnutrition was pervasive, but solutions were also difficult.

That evening, Tawab and Naderah shared what they learned over the last two weeks. Naderah had interviewed women at every chance, including at a local wedding. What she heard distressed her and was painful for me to hear. We talked through each situation and then of possible program development. Although the stories were about individuals, they reflected a community of shared pain.

In one story, a young girl had tried to kill herself because her family expected her to marry a very old man. She poured kerosene over herself and lit it. She died from severe burns over much of her body. Tawab heard another side of the same story when a local pharmacist he interviewed related the case to him. The father had come into the pharmacy for help because his daughter was badly burned. The pharmacist told him to take her to a doctor, but the father said he wouldn't because it would cost too much money. In Afghanistan, pharmacists dispense medications and recommend treatment without medical training or doctors' prescriptions. The father begged the pharmacist to come to his home and treat his daughter. When the man arrived at the house, he found the girl badly burned. She told him she wanted to make her dad pay for selling her off to an old man for the money. Now her father would have to return the money and pay for her hospital care. Yet, her father refused to take her to be treated, and she died shortly thereafter. In the end, her father had to repay the money or give another, even younger, daughter to the man.

In spite of the terrible economic toll the oppressive Taliban restrictions had on people, polygyny (a husband having more than one wife) seemed to be on the increase. In Afghanistan the groom's family paid the full costs of a wedding, including giving an agreed upon payment, either in cash or property, to the bride or, most often, to her family. It was not uncommon for poor people to describe these arrangements as "selling their daughters" and say that it meant that the rest of the family would have money to survive. Few daughters in these situations married willingly, though most accepted their fate and went quietly, as required in their society. What we found in our small study, which was supported by subsequent interviews, was that even though men could not afford more mouths to feed, they were marrying young girls—sometimes as young as nine or ten. In another study, a poor man told us that he did not have money to feed his children properly, or to send them to school. But, when asked what he would do if he did have the money, he said he would spend it to buy another wife. In most cases, such marriages caused great emotional pain to the girl and the other wife/wives. These young brides were committing suicide in greater numbers at that time, and every family we interviewed knew someone who had committed suicide or attempted it because of such a marriage.

The IDP Camp

By my fourth day I was feeling the oppression of the Taliban and the strain under which people lived. On this day, I saw the horrible conditions in the IDP camps. Under international agreements, the UNHCR (United Nations High Commissioner for Refugees) was limited to helping only those people who crossed international borders. IDPs were to be cared for by their own governments, but the Taliban government was not organized enough to govern or to provide aid. In addition, they limited who could bring aid and how it was distributed. The WFP was the main provider of food to IDPs, usually working through local partners. I visited Maslakh Camp,[11] the largest IDP camp in the area, with between 200,000 and 300,000 persons, most of whom were unemployed and in need of all services (WHO 2001).

A CHA doctor and the manager of their local development programs picked me up at my guesthouse and we drove directly to the camp, which was situated on a very dusty plain beside a gravel road just beyond the city. As we drove into this huge camp, we saw rows and rows of tents; there were no trees but rocks and gravel were everywhere. It was the bleakest place imaginable. Unlike the smaller, older camp I visited on the first day, with its various aid programs, this one was remote enough to create additional hardship, as people struggled to find ways to support their families. In spite of international efforts to provide for people's needs here, the Taliban used this camp as a bargaining chip in furthering their own agendas. In the end, local and international NGOs were often forced to give concessions to the Taliban for the "right" to provide services to these IDPs.

As we entered the camp, we stopped first at a small primary health clinic. It was busy, and the staff saw hundreds of people each day. Most of the camp was on the right as we entered the area and the clinic was on the left across a very dusty road. The clinic stood behind a tall wall, both for protection and privacy. As we entered through the doors, a guard checked us and gave us visitors' passes. The compound was filled with people, those who were sick and those who came with them. Everyone looked dusty and tired, weary and hungry. Their clothes were ragged. Long lines led into the clinic's rooms where doctors sat behind desks, seeing 100 patients an hour. The doctors looked as tired as their patients. Most of their patients were suffering from upper respiratory problems (from the dust), intestinal disorders, and/or malnutrition.

Next we drove further into the camp, to the edge of a series of tents, leaving the car to talk to those who lived there. Families arrived with almost nothing, and most were nearly starved. One tent was allotted to a family, and a local kitchen supplied one high-energy meal of porridge made of soy and corn flours per day per child. The food looked terrible, but it provided the necessary protein for a growing child. Yet, the whole family was hungry; therefore, this meal was divided among all family members. In this culture, you cannot eat if someone next to you is hungry. This meant no one had enough to eat. One woman told me: "We have nothing to eat but dust."

Some families had been living in the tents for six months or more, others for only three. There were new arrivals daily. It's almost impossible to describe the bleakness of the tent camps. Most tents were crudely constructed with canvas, but others were made from old blankets thrown over ropes and polls. Once-bright colors of the cloth were bleached by the sun and scoured by the winds. All the tents looked like the slightest wind would blow them over, but they seemed to withstand the gale winds that blew for 100 days each summer. Each family, regardless of size, shared a single tent, and each tent touched the one next to it.

One man, the head of an extended family of about 50 people who lived together in the camp, told us that one of his two wives was very sick and that five of his children had died since they came here six months ago. Someone brought us a baby dying of hunger because her mother died when she was born. There was no one to nurse her, and the family had no access to money to buy formula. Even if they had money for the food, they had no way to get to shops to buy it. And if they found the formula, the water they mixed it with was polluted. But they had none of that, instead they were feeding the child watered-down flour—a kind of gravy. The baby was too weak to cry, barely moving as it lay in my arms.

As we talked about the problems people faced, another family asked the CHA doctor to see someone in their family, a woman who was very sick, possibly with typhus. They complained that they took her to the clinic we had just visited but were given outdated drugs that did not work. They also said the doctors there would not give them all the drugs they needed. This was a common complaint. People judged doctors not by how much time they spent with a patient but by how many different medicines they prescribed. Regardless of the health problem, most local doctors in private clinics prescribed a tranquilizer, an analgesic, vitamin B_{12}, and an antibiotic for almost every illness. Because the local clinic across the road followed international standards, these people did not get this mix of medications and felt they were not well served. They told us that without help from a "real" hospital the woman would die.

We spent several hours visiting people in this camp and as we were leaving the family of the sick woman came to us again. They carried her as she hung limp between their arms; she was too weak to stand on her own. They challenged us to prove that we were there to help them by taking this woman to a hospital in town. We were trapped in a dilemma that had no positive way out. Unfortunately, to transport even a very ill woman in the NGO car could get the Afghan staff of CHA in terrible trouble with the Taliban if we were stopped at a check post. And there were many Taliban between here and the city. I could not make the decision as I was a visitor, and if we were caught, I was unlikely to suffer. Also, if stopped by the Taliban, the woman's family would be at risk as well. If they sent her with us and did not provide an escort, we would all be in even greater trouble. I asked the doctor who was in charge of this trip if we could help, but he said no. We drove away, proving to the people in the camp that we could not really help them in a way that they wanted to be helped. I carried this image with me for years, blaming myself for leaving the woman behind. I never learned what happened to her.

As we drove back to town I was feeling miserable and could not get the images of the woman and the starving baby out of my mind. To this day I wonder if we should have been braver and taken the risk to help the sick woman. The doctor took my reaction to mean that this must have been my first trip to an IDP camp, even though it was not in either Afghanistan or Pakistan. While sitting in the tent with these people, I knew they had expectations that we might be able to help and make a difference in their lives. Instead, I felt like we had wasted their time and raised their hopes.

I wanted to cry but did not want anyone to see me succumb. Somehow it felt like I had been less than human, listening to the horror stories, writing down what people said, but doing nothing to help. I heard their stories of loss; I held the dying baby but did not cry, not then. I was changed by this encounter. It shook me to my core. I had to grapple with my own inner turmoil: wanting to help people deal with the mental trauma of war and loss, yet knowing that the money used to do this might take away from other critical services like food, water, shelter, or medicine. My feelings at that time were of hopelessness and helplessness. I was starting to pull back from the problems of others, afraid to ask them questions, because I was afraid to face their answers. This was an indication that I needed to stop and reflect. I needed a day off, to think and to Focus, to feel grounded again.

Life was difficult under the Taliban, and those trying to provide aid often endured harassment or violence. They could easily be physically trapped between opposing sides in the war. While I was in Herat, two doctors, a husband–wife team who ran a rural clinic, were caught in the crossfire of a battle between the Taliban and another group. They survived, but suffered from nightmares for months afterward. Yet, the fighting was not always the most devastating thing they faced. I spoke to another doctor who had come to the office in Herat from Ghor for a few days rest, before returning to his clinic there. He told me that most people had left the area around Ghor, some because of the fighting, but most because of the drought. Those who stayed behind had no food and were waiting for the WFP to bring it. The worst part of all of this was that this doctor felt helpless. He did not want to return to Ghor, but his boss at CHA in Herat gave him no choice. In the midst of his own anguish, he empathized with how I felt about the IDPs I had seen in the Maslakh camp. He described Maslakh as the worst of the worst and stated that there was not enough help to make a difference. He was discouraged. And with this, I understood why CHA's director wanted me to have this trip and to see what his staff faced on a daily basis. He was determined to have a mental health program that could help his staff cope with hardship and constant contact with incredible human suffering. My job was really to help "the helper" (Omidian 2001).

Reflections

That night back at the guesthouse I reflected on the day. I was amazed at the level of resistance ordinary people had to the many restrictive edicts the Taliban used to control every aspect of their lives. So many of the people I had met were willing to risk life and limb and frequently did so in order to maintain their identity, of self and family. Often, they asserted their sense of their culture, with hope for the future—humans have an immense capacity for hope and caring. The Afghans lived under incredible strain. Yet their resiliency was apparent in the ways they kept hope alive, even when it meant taking risks—such as by painting beautifully evocative pictures.

The children of Herat had much to fear. They were warned to hide from the Taliban and to fear them. The kids I met were afraid of being beaten for going to school and trying to learn to read. They lived in fear of the sticks the Taliban carried. And they were afraid of the war that was close by (less than 80 miles away). These children were afraid of the drought because they knew their parents were worried. While I was there, no water had come through the city pipes in ten days, and the children had to haul buckets of water from central wells—from those that still had water.

Maybe the trip was a success after all. As I sat in a car at the airport waiting for the ICRC plane to arrive, I experienced again the resiliency of the Afghans. It was quiet with very few people around: just two ICRC cars and about eight people in our group. We saw a few Taliban wandering around the airport parking lot and the surrounding buildings. Most were young and all wore their characteristic messy, oversized black turbans. I heard only the wind and a radio tuned to Iran. Not only were we waiting for the plane, we were waiting while ICRC tried to find the man who stamped the passports. They sent cars out to find him, but he was not in his office or at his home.

After an hour of waiting, one of the drivers began to sing. He belted out songs at the top of his lungs, not caring if the Taliban heard him. He sang an aria from an Italian opera, followed by a Russian drinking song, next an Afghan love song, only to return to another Russian song. Between songs he told me that when life got too hard for him, he had to sing. He was a musician and singer, as was his wife. It turned out that he was the son of a woman who had been interviewed by Veronica Doubleday and highlighted in her book: *Three Women of Herat* (1990). He loved music and told me that he had spent one million Afghanis (years ago when money still had value) to buy a beautiful grand piano. He was close to tears as he described how the Taliban chopped it to pieces when they raided his house soon after they came to Herat.

The plane finally arrived, but the man never showed up to stamp our passports with exit visas. Over the five days I had spent here I only briefly saw the area and its needs. I spoke with office staff and their families, with clinic staff, and with teachers and students in home schools. The camps were the worst part of the trip— bereft of services, stuck out on a harsh rocky plain, the epitome of destitution. I saw children dying of starvation while parents looked on helplessly. They had no resources to change the situation in which they found themselves. People were depressed, tired of struggling, and afraid. I heard stories of striving and courage, of despair and loss. But it took courage to confront day-to-day life here.

Chapter 4

Hospitality Is Not Safe

*H*ospitality is an important part of Afghan culture. Regardless of the ethnic group, a good person or family is defined by their ability to take care of their guests. It is shameful to mistreat a guest, send one away, or fail to provide for one. Even in the poorest of homes, a guest will get the very best the family has. How one treated a guest was impacted by the Taliban, who strictly forbade foreigners from visiting Afghans at home. This edict caused many problems for my friends and me.

Meeting a Friend in Kabul

On my last day in Kabul, before I returned to Peshawar, I visited the UN Club. A crafts sale, representing various programs for women from around the country, was being held. Most NGOs had samples of local handicrafts to sell to the expat community, and I bought quite a few items. As I wandered through the rooms looking at the varied displays of embroidery or silk weaving, I noticed a young Afghan man. He followed me and finally started to talk to me. He first asked why I had come to Kabul and how I was. I knew that I knew him, but I could not place him. Then it hit me! Mansur! I realized that this was a man I had seen several times in Peshawar at Mohammad Beg's home. I had first met Mansur in 1988 when I visited a refugee work program in Pakistan. I was so embarrassed for not recognizing him that I must have turned bright red.

In typical Afghan style, Mansur invited me to be a guest at his home that evening and promised to have me back by the 9:00 PM curfew, which was strictly enforced. He may have extended the invitation out of politeness, not expecting me to accept, or he may not have realized the potential problems that could be created by my visiting his family in Kabul. Like me, he was a visitor here and was also based in Peshawar. I knew this family so well that I wanted to see them. Even more, I was lonely for people with whom I felt comfortable. I was unaccustomed to hanging out with expats, and, as an anthropologist, I wanted to see what life was like for Afghans. I automatically agreed to dinner at his sister's house, and we arranged to meet at 7:00 PM at the Club. In my desire to be with Afghans, I never stopped to consider my actions. Nor did I remember where he said we would be going. It never even occurred to me that there could be a problem.

As I was leaving for the staff house (I would return to meet him at 7:00 PM) he asked me if I had a chadari to wear. No, I didn't. He said he would bring his sister's. That should have triggered the warning bell in my head, but it didn't. Later, when I told Geri that Mansur wanted me to wear a chadari, she told me that under no circumstances could I wear one in Kabul. Only Afghan women wore them. If the Taliban saw a chadari woman in an NGO vehicle, it would be stopped and the driver arrested and beaten. They would interpret my wearing one as spying on them—getting everyone in deep trouble.

That evening, when the SAVE driver and I arrived at the UN Club, I moved to the backseat so that Mansur could sit in front, less problematic for them if the V&V stopped us. Mansur told the driver where we were going and handed me his sister's chadari, which I refused with an explanation. The driver was obviously not happy about something, but he remained quiet. We drove to a section of the city where there were absolutely no cars and ended up driving down a very rough dirt road guarded on both ends by the Taliban. Mansur told me this was why he wanted me to wear the chadari. The smart thing to have done at this point would have been for us to cancel the visit and for me to return to the staff house. I was so eager to visit an Afghan home, that I failed to see the risk to Mansur's family, who, as Afghans, were obligated to take care of their guest regardless of the danger to themselves.

When the car stopped, Mansur instructed the driver to pick me up at 8:30 so that I could be back at the guesthouse by the 9:00 PM curfew. We got out quickly and rushed into the compound, without looking right or left. In the compound I was warmly welcomed and treated like royalty. We walked through a rough, muddy garden to the house at the back of the compound. Mansur's sister, the mother of a large family, was very kind. One child, clearly with Down's syndrome, was obviously well loved and warmly cared for by all the other children.

Every time there was a knock at the door of the compound Mansur stiffened. But as each visitor entered the house and greeted people, he relaxed a bit. It took these nervous responses for me to finally realize what I had done. I felt terrible that I had put him and his family in danger. We tried to enjoy the evening but found it difficult until Mansur's brother-in-law arrived. At that point, he finally relaxed. This was an older man with turban and beard, looking very serious, yet he had an easy confidence. He immediately sat and started eating with us, although we had just finished the very tasty rice dish. He was two bites into his dinner when he stopped and looked at Mansur and me. He grinned and said that since there were no Taliban to see him he did not need to continue to wear his turban. He ripped it off his head and threw it to the side of the room with a flourish. His action broke any tension that remained in the room and the evening ended in warmth and friendship. After this, the family showed off their hidden TV, VCR, radios, and tape players. We laughed as they told stories of near misses with the Taliban and with life in general. I am sure my visit became one of their stories of disobedience and, luckily for all of us, another near miss.

At 8:25 the driver returned. As there were no other cars in the area, we could hear it over our conversation. It was amazing how quiet a city of a million people could be when there was a curfew and a ban on all music and television. With the driver waiting, I left the home quickly after hasty good-byes to everyone.

As we drove off the driver started in on me—and I deserved it. He asked me first if I spoke any Dari. He then asked me questions about where I was from and where I learned his language. I answered and we talked about unimportant things for a few minutes. He was only warming up as he assessed how much Dari I understood. He had something he needed me to know. He was jumpy and told me that I was never to come to this area after dark. Even though foreigners were allowed out until curfew at 9:00 PM, the area I was in was filled with "bad people" who were still fighting (meaning followers of rival warlords were trying to gain control here). Because of this, the Taliban maintained a strong presence. He said it was OK if I visited these people during the day, but I could never go there after dark. He told me in no uncertain terms that my friends should have known better, and if he had known ahead of time where I wanted to go, he would have told John to stop me.

I listened. Why was he getting mad at me now? I had no way of knowing this ahead of time. I needed everyone's guidance and was dependent on them to tell me these things. I looked back at the afternoon and realized that the invitation was impulsively offered and maybe only for politeness. Once I had agreed to come, there was no way Mansur could uninvite me. He was trapped by his own standards of hospitality. And because the driver was not warned beforehand, he did not feel he could stop me, a foreigner, either. I realized too late that I had to pay very careful attention to the subtleties of the situation.

Herat

By the summer of 2001, everyone in Afghanistan was fed up with the Taliban. In Herat, the Taliban were reacting to Western criticism and local opposition by becoming increasingly brutal. Pressure from the West to relax their edicts and change their policy toward women and children only increased their mistrust and heightened tensions. Because of this, foreigners could stay only in official staff houses for the international NGOs working in the area. Visitors like me had to stay at the UN guesthouse. And this place was usually fully booked.

My arrival in Herat turned out to be less stressful than I expected, compared to my other trips. After my arrival, the ICRC car took me to their compound in the city, where I was picked up by the CHA driver and taken immediately to the home of the head of CHA's Herat office, Dr. Saeed, to freshen up, eat, and meet Naderah, who was waiting there for me. The food was great and the home was lovely. It was cooled in the traditional Herati style, through wind-catchers on the roof that pulled in the fresh air to circulate within the house. Herat had 100 days of wind each summer, very dusty and drying, but traditional houses were designed to make a positive use of the wind to cool their rooms. And, this method was less dusty than opening windows.

We sat on red carpet covered mats on the floor and devoured a huge lunch of grilled eggplant with a garlic and yogurt sauce, bulani (a large flat pancake-like bread that is folded over and filled with potato or leeks before it is fried), and many meat dishes that I, as a vegetarian, did not eat. Dessert was fresh watermelon. It was wonderfully enjoyable. And the conversation was light, refreshing, and as caring as one would expect in an Afghan home. I spent the afternoon and the night there.

The next morning I said good-bye to Naderah and Tawab, who were flying back to Peshawar by way of Kabul. The plan was for me to go to the office followed by a visit with MSF and then return to have lunch with Dr. Saeed's family. When I arrived at the office, Dr. Saeed shyly told me that his family would be attending a wedding for several days and would not be available. This was a polite way to disinvite me, and I could see he felt terrible about it. Although Taliban edicts forbade foreigners from staying in Afghan homes, last night Afghan hospitality had overridden the Saeed family's own sense of personal security. Today, the office manager forced us all to be realistic. It was too dangerous for everyone.

My very presence could endanger my friends. Though the Taliban were unlikely to punish me for my transgressions, they could be brutal toward my Afghan friends and colleagues. I remembered my mistakes in Kabul several years before and willingly went to the UN guesthouse. I wanted to interview Afghan families so that I could understand their lives under the Taliban and to get a feel for the place, but my access to them would come only by using stealth. But with interviews and access being restricted, at this point I wondered how I would manage to do my job.

A large part of that first morning was spent on logistics for the rest of my stay. I had to check into the UN guesthouse (the only place in town for visiting foreigners). Dr. Saeed, the kindest and quietest of men, took me there. He felt so bad about being forced to make me leave his home that he did not want to make me wait alone in the garden as a room was arranged for me. Yet, we discovered that by sitting together in the garden we broke yet another rule. Afghans who did not work at the guesthouse were not allowed inside the compound—Taliban edict. The garden was a lovely quiet place in the midst of a very busy and noisy city. Tall pine trees hugged the perimeter and almost hid the high boundary wall and the razor wire that topped it. Roses bloomed in neat plots, and the large grassy area was kept trimmed. It took almost an hour before I was admitted into the building and shown to my room, small and dark and unfortunately right over the huge generator that ran most of the night and kept me awake. But I did not complain; the guesthouse staff had found space for me with no advance notice.

The following morning was a Friday, the Muslim day of rest, so shops and offices were closed. I participated in another act of defiance as yet another family disobeyed a Taliban edict in favor of Afghan hospitality—I was to be the guest of Wakil (the office manager) and his family. He did not take me directly to his house, in case there were Taliban watching. By this time I realized that, although one was at risk of being stopped by the Taliban, one was more likely to be caught by accident, as they were extremely disorganized. First, Wakil picked me up from the guesthouse in an office car and drove me to the CHA men's guesthouse (men had few of the restrictions that women faced). I was amused and curious why we came here but it was quickly apparent. There was no problem with me meeting or working with men, as a foreign woman. Taliban edicts were designed to keep me from meeting women. The Taliban would not stop me from entering this area, as they knew no women (other than I) were here. We walked through the compound and the building, out the back door, through the back gate, and down a long, winding alley to his home. This was much less conspicuous, and anyone watching the front of the guesthouse would assume I was still there.

Finally, I was in the home of a traditional Herati family. Their dialect was so different from the Kabul dialect, which I spoke, that I could barely understand what they said. Wakil told me a bit about his family. He and his wife lived next door to his four brothers and ten sisters— from three mothers. They preferred living in close proximity to each other.

One sister, age 27, had only three years of school. During the war against the Soviets, her mother wanted to keep her at home for safety. Wakil explained that this was in the early years of the war, which no one expected to continue for long. Herat was a city that valued education. Even though it was conservative, many women were highly educated. But the war changed that pattern, and as the following generations were unable to attend school, women's literacy rates plummeted. His nieces were all uneducated as they left school when the Taliban came. This left two generations of uneducated women in a community that had prided itself on the arts, music, and education before the wars started.

When Wakil left the room, the women talked to me about how difficult it was to be home all the time and how this made their lives nearly unbearable. They wanted the option to work outside of the home and to have their daughters educated. The issue was that of options and who had the right to decide: even those who were against education for girls felt that it was the family, not the Taliban, who should make this decision. And this was their feeling about all of the Taliban's edicts: it was the family that should decide for itself, as a unit.

One brother's wife showed signs of depression and anxiety. Every week she would go to a doctor for treatment and medicine. She said she took pills each day and complained of stomach trouble. She told me that if she stayed on a special diet she felt much better—a diet with no oil, salt, pepper, tomatoes, onions, or spices. But there was no joy in that, and she felt she couldn't cook separate food for herself. She also said her body hurt all over and that she felt pain in her arms like fire one time, or a severe headache another time, or legs aching very badly yet another. Her family told her it was *asaabi* (a local term for anxiety), but they had no idea how to help her. What she described were the typical signs of depression of which many women I interviewed over the years complained.

Lunch was excellent, and of course the women cooked more than needed for the number of guests. As usual, my being a vegetarian confused them. I always told people that I was following doctor's orders. Only then did they stop pushing me to eat meat. In Afghan culture, most illnesses had some kind of food restriction, and meat was commonly restricted for problems of the liver. I let them think whatever they wanted, as long as I did not have to eat the meat.

Reflections

I was constantly amazed at the level of resistance to the restrictive edicts the Taliban enacted to control every aspect of people's lives. The people who could afford it were willing to risk being jailed or beaten just to own and watch TVs and VCRs. Listening to music and films on VCRs became a form of protest. The more days they managed without being caught, the bolder they became. They would have music parties in their homes. People told me stories of wedding parties where the women would be in the back of the house having a traditional music party, drums and all. They would close all windows and doors to keep the sounds of the music from escaping. The room would become hot and stuffy from all the women packed in, trying to dance and celebrate. If the Taliban found out, the women's male relatives could be beaten for this infraction. Yet the music, like taking care of guests, was worth the risk. This showed spirit, but at a cost. It meant that even one's home was not safe.

Hospitality is a core value for Afghans, and it was one that the Taliban were not able to control, try as they might. So many of the people I met were willing to risk life and limb and did so very often in order to maintain the value of hospitality in all its nuances. Mostly, they wanted to maintain their sense of themselves and their culture with hope that things would be better in the future. These families took me in as a guest in spite of the risk. The Afghans had many ways of coping with life under an incredibly repressive regime. Yet, their resiliency was apparent in the ways they kept hope and social connections alive, even when it meant taking risks. Hospitality is not unique to the Afghans, but it is an internal marker of status and respect. Even the poorest Afghans, who have absolutely nothing to offer, will figure out a way to offer what they can to a guest. Over the course of my travels, I have sat in homes where the family could not afford more than bread and tea, yet they gave me tea with sugar to sip as we talked. The Taliban edicts against foreigners visiting in Afghan homes went against a cultural value that could not be set aside. I suspect that some Afghans, like Wakil, used this opportunity to quietly resist the regime they hated.

The Taliban were also imbued with the same cultural norm of hospitality. This was best exemplified by their inability to turn Osama bin Laden over to the Americans in 2001. As a guest in their country, they were honor-bound to protect him against all attacks, even if it meant their death and the death of their families. There was no way they could break this trust. Guests are the gift from God and they could not dishonor that obligation. If bin Laden left their protection or offered to be turned over, they could have acquiesced with honor. But Afghans will stop being hospitable and will turn their backs on their guests "when bamboo bloom."

Chapter 5

Programs

Applying Anthropology

As a consultant, one of my responsibilities was being accountable to the organization (often a donor agency) that paid me. As I think back to my time in Afghanistan, I realize that I had very few conflicts with the agencies that paid my salaries. But I often had to negotiate through a maze of conflicting agendas. As an applied anthropologist I often answered to more than one boss. In many cases, I was hired by an agency to fulfill a contract. At the same time, I had to be responsible to their donors, who might have their own objectives. In any case, I had to be aware of the politics of the situation and try to avoid any pitfall that might emerge in the course of the work. And, maybe most important, I had to be honest about the data collected and try to include accurate and complete information in my reports, regardless of how the donor or agency felt. For example, there were times when I was asked to remove or change information. I had a policy of refusal. I could add an addendum that noted any concerns, but the data stood as collected.

Shuhada and Novib: To Whom Did I Report?

The work with Shuhada Organization was difficult for many reasons: travel, security, and logistics (as noted previously). But there was also tension between the head of Shuhada Organization and me, because I had to answer to several levels of stakeholders. In this case, I was hired by Novib to study the strengths and weaknesses of Shuhada, always a task that caused apprehension on the part of the agency. I also needed to write a report that Shuhada could use to improve or enhance its programs for its beneficiaries. Finally, I had to honor the people in Afghanistan whom we had interviewed. Their voices needed to be heard through my report.

Shuhada Organization was among only a small number of agencies that worked in the remote areas of Hazarajat at that time. Shuhada staff managed under harsh conditions and often with few resources. As a minority group, the Hazara staff of the organization were at risk of harassment, beatings, and/or imprisonment by the Taliban. As noted above, the year the Taliban pulled out of Yakawlang, they gathered a large group of men together, shooting and killing them all. Members of Shuhada's staff were among those killed. The risks were real, the conditions were harsh, and the work was difficult. Understandably, the head of Shuhada wanted to support her staff and defend her programs.

As I was not able to be part of the actual survey process, I could not double-check any of the results. In the findings, there were several areas in which I suspected the data to be incorrect or where the surveyors should have probed for more details. I noticed instances of glaring gaps between the questions asked and the answers that generated the data. Overall, however, the data collected by the teams showed both strengths and weaknesses in programming for both the health and education sectors. Thus, my report on these sectors of Shuhada was basically positive, but had no problems been noted, one would have assumed that the information was inaccurate.

The biggest problems came because of Shuhada's relations with the Taliban, both as Hazaras and as aid providers; these problems were out of Shuhada's control. As noted in chapter 2, doctors and other staff were often imprisoned or beaten as they tried to travel to Pakistan for further training. Their movements were restricted. As an NGO, Shuhada was forced to pay bribes in order to keep working. In addition, it sometimes lost equipment to Taliban officials. In Yakawlang, for example, the hospital had a generator but the local Taliban commander demanded that the hospital give him electricity from its generator. The hospital decided not to use the generator because it was expensive to run, and giving electricity to the Taliban commander gained nothing for the organization. Thus, I noted in the report that, according to the doctors surveyed, the lack of a generator created a problem for the hospital, as the electricity was needed to run the lights during surgery. My report, therefore, was taken as criticism (which it was) instead of being used to generate needed solutions to the generator/electricity problem. Although I could understand Shuhada's reaction, because it had lost a lot of equipment and money to the Taliban, the hospital absolutely needed a generator, and had it informed its donor, there might have been more help. I discovered how common it was for small agencies, like Shuhada, to try to hide their problems from donors, when they could have acted to educate them instead.

In the education sector there were many problems for the community in trying to keep boys in school. Although families wanted both boys and girls in school, and the Taliban tried to block all girls' schools, Shuhada had many programs throughout Hazarajat, but most had to be operated in secret. The situation was dangerous for the organization, the teachers, and the children. Shuhada used very innovative ways to ensure community support and cooperation, which made the schools safer, because the Taliban were less vindictive when the village elders supported a program. Schools were held under trees or in dirt-floored buildings, often with shortages of books or desks or any other kind of equipment. Yet, schools were open, and the number of children who attended was amazing.

That each family would give seven kilograms of wheat directly to the teacher of each boy in school illustrated how important education was in this area. Also important was how this method encouraged cooperation between the community and the school. Yet, in the survey almost all male teachers and families with boys in school stated that the drought was causing great economic hardship. Because of this, many boys were no longer able to attend school. In every school, numbers were dropping as families had to pull their sons out when they could no longer pay the wheat to the teacher. And because the teachers were not receiving pay, they had to quit teaching in order to earn a livelihood for their own families. In the report, I tried to show this problem in a way that was uncritical of Shuhada, yet in a way that would point to an area in need of more thought and maybe more donor money (with the funder of this survey the most likely candidate). Indeed, the situation was critical, and any solution would have been difficult to carry out.

While there were problems of paying salaries, the physical structure of the schools, and obtaining books for boys' schools, the girls' schools had that and more. For girls' schools, and with home schools in Kabul, the only way to stay safe was to stay hidden or create other deceptions. Shuhada often did both. This was the area of greatest conflict with the Taliban. And again, Shuhada managed to come up with innovative solutions. They paid the women teachers a higher salary, and they disguised the classrooms so that the Taliban would not close the schools. This worked well during the school year, but left teachers without income over the winter months. One woman teacher told us that, because she was so poor, her own children could not attend school. For me, that highlighted the need for greater donor investment in these programs, but this caused yet another area of contention with Shuhada's director, and I was asked to change the report.

My report, according to notes from Novib, was one of the most positive they had ever received. Yet, the head of Shuhada protested its results and wanted many of the findings deleted. I had to answer to Novib, yet find a way to honor Shuhada Organization, but mostly I needed to honor the people in the field. This meant my report had to reflect what we found in the field, based on the information provided by those interviewed, and not what the agency wanted to show. At the same time, I knew that the agency had legitimate concerns. In part, the tension was because program needs could not be met in the current political situation, which could bring reprisals by the Taliban against the organization. That did not change the fact that those needs existed. It was a hard sell to Shuhada. The Shuhada management saw the responses from stakeholders as misunderstandings or as trivial complaints in the broader scheme of things. Some of the problems needed to be identified, possibly for future action, but could not be solved under the current structure of the organization at the time. In fact, the complaints gave indications of areas where services might need improvement, rather than actual weaknesses in the agency.

In the end, both the donor and the agency accepted the report. We moved forward to consider how to implement some of changes that came from the strategic planning meetings that followed the report. By the end of the contract, I had an even deeper respect for Shuhada and its entire staff, from the head of the agency to the woman who cleaned my room in Jaghori, from the doctors and teachers to the students who attended their classes. In the world of post-9/11 Afghanistan, Shuhada Organization has been able to expand its programs into even more remote areas. Thanks in part to the dedication of this and other organizations, the Hazara maintain an enthusiasm for education for their daughters and sons. Nevertheless, the problem of access to these areas remains; roads have barely improved and the Taliban again control some of the roads that allow access into the region.

CHA: Starting a Mental Health Program

In contrast to my work with Shuhada Organization, my work for CHA had less tension between myself and the agency or donor, in part because the director of CHA hired me from a general fund within the agency—a fund that was not tied to a particular outcome. As an organization, it wanted me to use the information I compiled to develop a psychosocial wellness program. Because I was employed directly by CHA, I was able to be a partner with it and was seen as an insider.

As Afghan aid workers moved in and out of their program areas, mostly in western Afghanistan, they had to respond to various emergencies, including drought, earthquakes, war, and epidemics. CHA programs always included infrastructural development, agriculture, health, and education, as a holistic approach to working with war-ravaged communities. When interviewed, staff noted that they saw their work take hold and begin to show results, only to have the next wave of war, disaster, or some government edict erase all that they had accomplished. It was frustrating work. Whether they were male or female, these aid workers faced dangers, traumas, and frustrations in their work that had profound psychosocial ramifications.

Often, the Taliban would try to take some of the aid going to needy areas, diverting it to their own select areas of need, such as for their fighters in the north. CHA rarely gave aid handouts to areas that needed food. Instead, they worked with the WFP in "food for work" activities. For example, once a community had agreed to build a road (that would also help bring aid to their area) in exchange for WFP wheat. When the road was near completion, WFP shipped the wheat, only to have the Taliban seize it and send it to an area that was pro-Taliban. The community was close to revolt and blamed

CHA for stealing their wheat—putting the CHA local staff in danger. It took careful negotiation with the community and WFP to solve the problem. Unfortunately, this was a common occurrence.

CHA wanted me to help the staff address their own reactions to what they were doing and seeing around them. I was to set up a program that would provide debriefing in Peshawar after each trip to the field, as well as help Afghan staff as they lived as refugees outside their own country. This program was new to the agency and to the donors but was the brain-child of the head of the agency, who saw the need and found a way to cover the cost of a technical advisor in psychosocial wellness. It was an enormous task that might not get funded past the initial development period. At that time, donors and aid agencies tended to ignore psychosocial issues and focus on "real problems" like hunger and disease. In fact, it was three more years before the term "psychosocial" became a common word in development circles. When CHA and I were trying to develop a program, we felt isolated but hoped that a solid program with data to support us would convince donors of its value.

Initially, I was asked to *help the helpers*, yet I had to deal with my own reaction to my position. I could not help feeling that my salary, though it was lower than many of the Afghan department managers at CHA, took money away from possible services to people in Afghanistan. How could I justify it? I even asked myself if what I was doing was trying to make people feel good about being hungry—a ridiculous notion. The staff at CHA helped me overcome my trepidation by always making me feel welcome. As I grew to understand their struggle to work in Afghanistan and live in Pakistan, I came to understand that the healthier they were, the better they could do their work and take care of their families. They, like me, needed a way to cope with all they saw.

This was not an easy time. My skills had generally been used to conduct surveys, write reports, make recommendations, or facilitate trainings. The program that we hoped to develop needed to be culturally sensitive and distinct from clinical treatment. Mental illness was highly stigmatized; therefore, the program needed to address mental health issues in a way that would not be labeled as "psychiatric treatment." Yet, Afghan staff willingly talked about their need for some kind of help and support. The answers to questions I asked in surveys on this subject were personal and clearly related to both war experiences and problems in their current daily lives. I often did not have to seek out people to answer my questions; staff came to me, relieved to have someone with whom they could talk.

I was not trained as a psychologist, and I think, in the end, this helped. Because I did not have a clinical background, I had no preconceptions about the need for clinically based work. Instead, I had worked on the anthropology of emotions and community-based models of wellness for a number of years. I also knew that talk therapy was not something Afghans, or others from this region, appreciated. They wanted solutions to problems, or medication to remove their pain, or privacy so that no one would know what was wrong—or all three. What I did not know was which model would help the most. I could see an enormous need for a program to meet their needs, the kind that supported local, culturally defined resiliency. The difficulty was in how to implement such a program without medicalizing the processes.

This was when I called on a friend in Islamabad for help. Nina Joy Lawrence became my collaborator on this project and coauthor of articles on Focusing in Afghanistan. She was a licensed counselor who had the skills in psychology—a good match to mine. She had been taking courses in the United States on Focusing and was willing to teach it to Naderah, Tawab, and me. In turn, CHA's management staff were part of the first exploratory training we conducted. Their feedback helped us develop the program in a culturally appropriate and sensitive way. It was a process of learning a technique, translating it into local symbolic categories, and using appropriate metaphors and allegories. The program, with the help of Naderah and Tawab, grew to meet important criteria: it was sensitive to local Islamic models, supportive of Afghan resiliency, and allowed for privacy. Most felt it enhanced their connection to their religious roots in positive ways.

We quickly discovered that poetry and the sayings of the Prophet were important keys to this work. Nina started with a Rumi poem:

The Guest House
This being human is a guest house.
Every morning a new arrival.
A joy, a depression, a meanness,
some momentary awareness comes
as an unexpected visitor.
Welcome and entertain them all!
Even if they're a crowd of sorrows,
who violently sweep your house
empty of its furniture,
still, treat each guest honourably.
He may be clearing you out
for some new delight.
The dark thought, the shame, the malice,
meet them at the door laughing,
and invite them in.
Be grateful for whoever comes,
because each has been sent
as a guide from beyond.

(Barks 1997)

With this poem came discussions of what a guest means in Afghan society and how an Afghan takes pride in how he or she cares for a guest. Hospitality matters and the guest can expect the best of treatment, even if he or she was uninvited or unwanted. One Afghan told me that to treat a guest well brings blessings from Allah, but to treat an unwanted guest well brings double the blessings. I thought back to my visits to Afghan homes during this time and wondered how many blessings I helped people gain through my mistakes.

Focusing worked for the Afghans because it took the same attitude—kindness, respect, and a caring lack of judgment—about hospitality and applied it to individuals' internal responses to events in their lives. For people who dealt with war and displacement, much had happened that was traumatic, but how one muddled through mattered. Through Focusing we were able to develop a program that used local resiliency skills and Islamic notions to help people cope (Omidian and Lawrence 2008, 2007).

We presented some basic information to a group of Afghans and then helped them transform it into something meaningful for themselves. Poetry was an excellent way to transform theoretical information into something with which individuals could identify. So many Afghans were familiar with Jalaludin Balkhi (as they called Rumi), who was born in what became modern Afghanistan, and most could quote poetry that supported what we were trying to do. Many also gave us *hadeez* (sayings of the Prophet) that worked. We started collecting these to help us as we (Naderah, Tawab, and I) prepared to move to different locations in the field.

In Herat, Naderah, Tawab, and I used Focusing to help us cope with what we saw. For example, after telling me the stories they had collected on suicides, Naderah, Tawab, and I felt miserable, too numb to cry. We used Focusing (Focusing Institute 2003) to deal with our reactions, finding a way to handle all that we were subjected to from the responses collected in this survey. We sat together, quietly, but supporting each other by our presence. Each of us took turns to pay attention to those internal guests that came from all we saw: pain, sorrow, even horror and helplessness. Tawab went first and brought his full attention inside himself, to the pain he felt. He described his pain as a guest sitting in his heart and held that pain with kindness. It started to change on its own as he sat with it. First he described it as feeling like pressure on his heart; so next, he sat with the pressure. At this point, he said that the pressure started to leave, the way steam rises from a cup of tea, and he breathed it out of him. Soon, he sat back with a smile on his face. He had found his way to cope. Then, it was Naderah's turn. She also found relief after many tears slipped out and landed on her lap. Slowly she came back to the room, calmed and ready to return to work. Although we were all novices at this, we found it made a huge difference in our work. Once they left for Kabul, I found it hard to do Focusing when I was alone, though I used it alone later in Peshawar and in the United States. Nevertheless, the support of friends helping to hold the calm, caring space made a difference.

Chapter 6

Evacuation

Just as we were getting started with CHA's mental health program, 9/11 happened and the world tilted in a new direction. I think everyone, at least every American, remembers what they were doing on September 11 in 2001. I do. I had just returned to the home where I was staying in Peshawar from CHA, very tired, sweaty and hungry. The temperatures outside were well over 100°F and the temperature in my car was at least 120°. The drive from my office to my home was too short for the air conditioners to work. My only thought on arrival was to take a quick shower and get the dust of the city and the car off of me. It was about 5:00 PM in the evening. At that time I lived with an Afghan family and liked to spend part of my evenings helping the children with their English. It was a wonderful break after a day of planning around trauma and mental health concerns.

As I came down after my shower, I joined the kids who were doing their homework on the floor of the TV room. I noticed that the TV was on and tuned to CNN; I became aware of something strange about the show. It was worse than a bad B movie. I felt my stomach lurch. I had to read the banner across the bottom several times. I asked the children if it was some comedy channel that was doing a spoof. "No," they said, "that's CNN. Why?" I looked again. The headline read: "America under attack." When the words finally sank in, it felt like the whole world twisted on its axis and things were no longer standing upright. It was at this moment that I knew the world changed and would never be the same again. I watched in horror, surrounded by the now silent Afghan children, as the second airliner crashed into the World Trade Center. I continued to stare, oblivious to the world around me and watched as the towers fell in a rush of dust and debris. I continued to stare.

My cell phone rang, but it took a while to realize it. "Hello?" It was the head of CHA.

"Have you seen the news?" he asked. And I could hear the uncertainty and concern in his voice. "How are you?"

"Yes," (pause) "I'm watching CNN. Do you have any other news? What's going on?" I asked as I started to take in the reality of the situation.

He answered: "I'm not sure, but I do know that you have to stay at home until we tell you otherwise. Things might get violent if people rally to support this action. I think things could get dangerous in Peshawar so just stay home. Good thing you live with an Afghan family; you won't be as noticeable this way."

Had I lived with other expats, we might have been targeted.

Peshawar was known for riots and demonstrations that could turn violent. At that time there was strong support for the Taliban here. Many Pakistan military personnel who worked in Afghanistan and supported the Taliban lived in Peshawar. During the first Gulf War there had been riots in support of Iraq and against any foreigners. A Pakistani friend of mine told me that during that war he was driving through a mob with a foreigner in his car. He put a sign with a picture of Saddam Hussein in the car window so that the mob would leave him alone. When he was stopped he told the mob that the person with him was Muslim and supported Saddam Hussein. That was a very dangerous time.

This situation was equally dangerous. The children went to school the next day as normal. But when they came home, they were hesitant to look me in the eye. Many children in their school had fathers who worked in Afghanistan for the Pakistan army, and most of these families were pro-Taliban. They couldn't understand why Afghan children were against the Taliban when their own fathers were helping them. Few urban Afghans, who lived in Pakistan at that time, were pro-Taliban. They were in Pakistan because it was too dangerous for them to remain in their own country. Yet, they tried to find ways to travel there safely. Most Afghan men sported long beards, wore turbans, and managed to look like most men of the tribal region—both Pakistani and Afghan. Looks were deceiving.

Over the next three days I sat at home, waiting for news. Many times I tried calling friends around Peshawar to see how they were doing. I wasn't able to reach anyone. Each day the children brought me news from outside. It was a very uncertain time. By Friday I was frustrated, unable to reach my friends and trapped in the house. I tried again to contact my friends at one international agency. This time the secretary recognized my voice and told me: "Madam, why are you still here! There are no foreigners left in Peshawar! They left Tuesday night in a caravan to Islamabad. You should've gone with them!" I had not known this because I did not live within the expat community.

I was shocked and amazed. And suddenly I felt very alone. I tried calling the U.S. Consulate in Peshawar, but nobody answered. Next, I tried the embassy in Islamabad but couldn't get through. Finally, I called the Fulbright Foundation in Islamabad, and they answered on the first ring. I talked to the head of Fulbright, an American woman, who told me I should leave Peshawar as soon as possible. She couldn't recommend me staying there any longer, but she didn't want me going by road, either. At this point, I called the CHA office and talked to the director, telling him the news. We agreed that I should leave Pakistan immediately. Within hours, CHA had an airline ticket for me and I left that night for the United States. It was September 14.

There were lots of tears as I packed to leave, because none of us knew when I would return. Afghan friends came to the house to say goodbye, and the office gave me money to support me for the next few months. They told me if I needed more they would send it. Concern was etched on their faces because they knew what it was like to flee because of war or politics. We all knew the world had changed and we had no idea in which direction it would go. These wonderful people had fought long and hard against the Taliban and against the Soviets, but they were tired of fighting. They were hoping that this might stir the United States into renewed interest in Afghanistan: maybe bring a way to get the Taliban out and establish a stable government. That was a difficult road and it wasn't clear at this point if it could happen. At eight that evening I piled in a car for my drive across town to the airport. It was so hard to leave, because I didn't know if I could ever come back.

From Peshawar, I flew directly to Dubai where I transferred to a flight to Holland. In Holland I was lucky to get the last seat on a flight to one of the first U.S. airports to reopen. I was shaky, cold, and stressed. When the plane touched down in Nashville, the people on the plane erupted in applause and cheering. I was back on home soil, but unsure of the future and worried for my friends and colleagues in Pakistan. We had no idea what would happen next.

In the United States, as I waited to return to Pakistan and Afghanistan, I was in daily contact with friends, colleagues, and others in Peshawar. And almost daily I got letters asking me to find a way to encourage the United States to become involved in Afghanistan, to stop the Taliban, and to use force, as these Afghans felt it would be necessary. Many said that they were willing to lose their house if it would save their country. These were not words said lightly or in jest. Afghans were tired of war and wanted peace, but they wanted justice as well. They wanted a government that would represent them, all of them. And they wanted the Taliban and the warlords to answer for the human rights abuses of the last 20-plus years.

One of the letters I received illustrates Afghan reactions as the United States started fighting the Taliban. The writer, whom I will not name, wrote it as a prayer for the future:

> Last night when we heard the news of the attack, we felt a kind of relief that Taliban could not be spared. We prayed for the security of innocent people in Afghanistan and those forces conducting the attack. We prayed to Allah to keep them safe and unharmed. We wish them total success in their operation. We prayed to Allah to save humanity from the masters of terror and the terror itself.
>
> We hope to see this country a place of peace, a place where every human being can live, stay, work and travel with safety and honor. We ask Allah to return us our very basic rights in our country after such a long time. We ask Allah, as we have suffered so long, for a time of mercy. We ask Allah to save humanity. (October 15, 2001)

Every letter I received had the same theme, that the United States and the world help the Afghans rid themselves of this horror.

The Taliban left quickly to regroup in the border areas of Pakistan. By the end of 2001 it was clear that CHA could return to Kabul and establish offices there. Once the Taliban left Kabul, doctors returned there in droves— meaning they could finally leave the villages where they had worked for NGOs for the last five years and reopen their private clinics in urban areas. Suddenly there would be no clinics for rural families. Many rural schools, which had managed to survive drought and the Taliban, also closed. Their teachers found work in Kabul, Mazar-e-Sharif, or Herat. Even the city of Kandahar welcomed visitors, though areas outside the city remained dangerous. Like Afghanistan before the war, health and education services again became urban phenomena.

NGOs struggled to maintain their work in remote areas. The government was too weak to run basic services and was unable to meet its own payroll. At this time Shuhada was able to grow into a stronger organization and it was one of the few that maintained its programs in Pakistan. Quetta is still home to a large number of Hazaras, many of whom have Pakistan citizenship and access to Pakistani schools, universities, and health services. Shuhada remains one of the key NGOs that provide health and other services to them. In Bamyan, Shuhada now has close ties to the local government and is a conduit for many services.

CHA grew exponentially after 2001. It became one of the largest Afghan NGOs in the country, moving its head office to Kabul early in 2002, where I joined it when I returned from "exile." The mental health program remained unfunded, though we tried for another year to get it running. I was able to visit programs in Herat, Balkh, and Kandahar. To this day, CHA still has connections to the psychosocial program and to me.

Save the Children, U.S.; The International Rescue Committee (IRC); The American Friends Service Committee (AFSC); and UNICEF supported the psychosocial program in various ways, funding various trainings, particularly for teachers and schoolchildren. The psychosocial and Focusing program grew and changed. Several local NGOs and one international program use it as part of their service delivery. In 2005, it became part of an internship program for students of Kabul University.

Chapter 7

Conclusion

Dilemmas of Fieldwork

The Taliban changed as they entered new territories, and over time, they became more and more radical and brutal as the West turned against them and supported their enemies. The Taliban of Kabul in 1998 were growing and expanding their control. They seemed cocky and sure of themselves. A high-level Taliban in the Ministry of Public Health that first summer told me that he was not sure if he would be alive by the end of the year. He was a moderate who wanted peace for his country. He also wanted the country to recover from war and take its place among the nations of the world. At that time, there was an internal ideological struggle within the ranks of the Taliban, between the moderates and the ultra-conservatives. Unfortunately, the moderates lost.

In the summer of 2000, when I traveled by road to Ghazni from Quetta, those in charge of the Taliban were hard at work trying to contain and/or destroy the Hazara of the central highlands of Afghanistan. They were also struggling to maintain control of the country and to capture the last area that was holding out against them. Yet, by the fall of the same year along the same route, they seemed to be losing control. The countryside around Kandahar, their ethnic and political base in the south, was held at night by warlords and bandits.

When I flew to Herat in June of 2001, it was clear that the Taliban were trying to hold onto their areas through the brutal use of fear. Heratis coped by quiet opposition and through underground movements like "home schools." Even music was an act of defiance, as evidenced by the number of radios and cassette players I saw.

Through all this, the Afghans had to adapt to survive. These coping strategies started with the Soviet invasion. Families divided resources and loyal-

105

ties, as if to weather the political storms and the subsequent wars. By the time I arrived in Afghanistan on my first trip, those who had supported the communist party, or even one of the many warlords who fought the Soviet armies, were seen as enemies of the Taliban, and many were prevented from working. Others were jailed. It was common for an extended family to have one member who was a Taliban, and someone else who was a communist, and still another who fought with the mujahideen. Cross loyalties were as much about survival as they were about ideology. The old adage, "Don't keep all your eggs in one basket," fit the reality of managing the very dangerous political landscape, as decades of conflict constantly changed who was in power.

What struck me the most with each trip inside was the effort by ordinary Afghans to maintain their cultural values, including that of hospitality, and their amazing resiliency in the face of multiple hardships and trauma. As an anthropologist with a focus on mental health I was interested in the question of well-being, positive resiliency, and community wellness. I wanted to know why so many Afghans could lose so much—property, family members, or livelihood—and still laugh. What characteristic or trait did they possess that accounted for this? I returned to Afghanistan in December of 2001 and lived in Kabul for five years, looking at that question. These early experiences gave me many insights that I was able to study in greater depth later.

Aid work often occurs in dangerous places, and rules exist to help mitigate the danger and to keep both the expatriates and the local population with whom they work as safe as possible. Aid agencies, such as those for which I worked, maintained positions of neutrality on the ground whenever possible. Yet, aid work is inherently political, and it is important to take a stand, particularly in areas of human rights, women's rights, health rights, or children's rights, even though these are also contested spaces. Furthermore, aid agencies often act as information collectors of "on the ground" realities. They try to educate donors and or governments of the cultural, health, political, or human rights issues faced by the local populations. However, there is a fine line between information sharing to educate and information collection that can be classed as spying for a government. The slippery slope is one that can be hard to negotiate and thus must be treated very carefully, and with full awareness of that dilemma.

As an applied anthropologist, I was never impartial. I had an obligation to record and report what I saw in some very remote areas. I was not neutral, for I could not support the Taliban or their agenda. Yet, when I encountered individual members of the Taliban government, I could see that person as a human (with norms and values, as we all have) and find ways to meet him and listen to him. As the story from Jaghori points out, not every Taliban was talib.

Working in Afghanistan was not easy. Though I seldom felt personally at risk, there were many times when I was worried about the safety of those with whom I worked. As you read my accounts, I am sure you found many places where you questioned my actions. I am also sure others would have done many things differently, but hindsight and armchair reflections are of little help in those critical moments in the field. We work with people in real-life situations, often needing to make quick decisions. Our actions are based on the information we have at the time and the "feel" of the moment. It is often well after the event that its real meaning comes to light. Much like the therapist or medical doctor, our mandate is to "do no harm," but in a context of war and uncertainty, this is often very difficult. Sometimes just being present brings harm; other times, we are merely helpless in the face of the larger political reality.

This book highlights issues that arose for me as I worked as an applied anthropologist with various NGOs in Afghanistan, during the time that the Taliban controlled over 90 percent of the country. These stories illustrate the kinds of dilemmas I faced as a consultant, as I tried to fulfill contracts for which I was hired. Even more important to me than the contract or the obligations to the people or agency that hired me, was the need to honor the people I studied and to try to protect those with whom I worked from possible repercussions from my presence. My stories are grounded in the space between Afghans with whom I worked and for whom I worked, and the Taliban. The Taliban, even when absent, presented a force of fear in a space that was internationally contested.

Values, those of the anthropologist (mine) and those of the people with whom I worked, were often challenged. I was amazed at how my Afghan colleagues negotiated the gap between the dictates of their own culture and the harsh rules set by the Taliban. At the same time, I, as the anthropologist and outsider, had to negotiate between my own values and those of my hosts, as I tried to avoid being noticed by the Taliban.

Dusk at the shrine in Mazar-e-Sharif in northern Afghanistan. It is a major pilgrimage site for the Afghan Shia population. Photo taken in 2005.

As the war in Afghanistan intensifies again, I worry that the new Taliban, who are very different from those I met, will be even harder to engage in discussion. During the five-year period I lived in Afghanistan after 2001 and during the many trips I took inside after I left in 2007, I was struck by how hopeful Afghans were for peace to come and for a chance to live normal lives. Most had never seen a normal life, or rather, war was normal for them. But they want more. They want peace and justice. I am still in touch with Aziz and, through him, Engineer Muslim. We worked together for a number of years for the Quakers, with our office based in Kabul. Those were good times. But we often felt like we were watching night return, as the resurgence of the Taliban took back more and more of the country by force and through violence. Maybe the Afghans were right. Peace will come when bamboo bloom.

Postscript

$\mathcal{U}$pon one of my latter returns to Kabul, winter was at its most fierce, even though I had sworn I would never spend another winter day in that country's freezing clutches. Yet, here I was, back in that familiar airport—in the winter. There was a chaos and disorderliness about Kabul as it exploded with people and construction projects. The air was filled with dust and the soot of wood smoke from all the homes being warmed in the deepening winter. So far, the weather was manageable. Winter came late that year; usually by 15th November the ground was frozen and the rains had left small lakes of ice that made walking treacherous. Instead of ice, there were rockets and bombs, but not so many of those that people stayed inside their homes. My first week on this trip reminded me of how much I am connected to Afghans and to Afghanistan.

As I arrived, I felt more like an international tourist than an aid worker being carted to and fro. Flights arrived from Dubai, Islamabad, New Delhi, and Istanbul. Each promised an adventure. Stepping off the plane onto the tarmac that November day, I saw all the changes that had occurred since my last trip. There was a new airport terminal being built by the Japanese. The old terminal was also evolving. The building had been refurbished, painted in light colors; it felt airy and bright. There were new chairs on which to sit and officials greeted people with the warmth of Afghan hospitality. The lines for passport control and the booths where the officials sat showed an orderliness I had rarely seen. I wondered what had happened to the Afghanistan I knew. Then I walked through the doors behind passport control to the area where luggage arrived in the terminal and I saw that the external order I had just passed through was truly an illusion.

I stood with many other foreigners to get my police document stamped. Here, the pushiest always got served first. Finally, the man behind the counter noticed me and told his colleague to take me next. He recognized me from past trips and knew I spoke Dari. With the police document stamped, my next task was to wade through the jumble of luggage from the plane to find my suitcase. By that time all the unclaimed pieces were in a mound on the floor. It took a few moments but I spotted it! Buried under a pile of other, larger cases. I had no complaints: my luggage had arrived. Welcome to Kabul.

Appendix A

Survey Samples

Shuhada's Health and Education Services
Hazarajat, Afghanistan
July 2000

HEALTH PROGRAMMING

Hospitals:

1. What is your comment regarding the improvement of the hospital?

Community Comments:

1. From which areas are you?
2. How did you come to the hospital (transportation)?
3. Did the doctor visit you on time?
4. Did you get the medicine from the hospital?
   Why or why not?
5. Did you get the prescription for the medicine from outside the hospital?
6. How is the attitude of your doctor?
7. How was the attitude of the hospital personnel?
8. Do you get your meals on time?
9. What is your opinion of this health centre?
10. What is the benefit of this health centre in your life?
11. Do you have latrine and bathroom in your home?
12. Can you afford to buy medicine from the bazaar?
13. What are the diseases spread in your community?
14. Are there people to give injections in your area?
15. Proposals:

Hospital Administrators:

1. How many sections and beds does the hospital have?
2. What are the problems in your section of the hospital?
3. What do you propose to improve the work of the hospital?
4. Is there a registrar here?
5. Has your financial supervisor participated in professional workshops or not?
   If not, why not?

Nurses Questionnaire:
Male:
Female:

1. Which nursing courses did you complete?
2. How long have you working here?
3. Do you give health education to your patients?
   What?
4. What are the most common problems you see in your female patients?
5. Other Problems:
6. Expectations from Shuhada for clinic midwives and nurses:
7. Common diseases:

Pharmacy Questions:

1. Have you studied in the faculty of pharmacy?
2. What do you know about the danger and side effects of medicine?
3. Do you have enough medicine in your stock?
4. Are you able to get the important medicines that you need?
5. Can the patients afford the medicines they need?
6. Proposals:

Vaccinator Questions:

1. Which types of vaccines do you have in stock?
2. Whom do you vaccinate?
3. What are your problems regarding vaccines?
4. Are vaccination campaigns implemented?
5. Why or why not?
6. Do you have the routine childhood vaccines?
7. Where do you get your vaccines?
8. How do you keep your vaccines?
9. Proposals by Vaccinators:

Education Program:

Headmaster Interviews:

1. Gender:
2. In which month does school begin and when does it finish? How many months?
3. Are programs according to the Taliban curriculum?
4. Is the curriculum according to the level of the students?
5. Are you satisfied with the curriculum?
6. Which type(s) of curriculum do you use in the school?
7. Where do you get your teaching materials?
8. Do you have:
   a. laboratory
   b. map
   c. globe
   d. skeleton
9. What can Shuhada do to help you improve the education program?
10. Problems:
11. Surveyors' comments:

Teachers' Interviews:

1. Are you from the same area in which you are teaching or from another area?
2. Are the parents of your students cooperating with you in the process of teaching?
   Explanation?
3. Why did you choose to be a teacher?
4. Which subjects are you interested in (do you like the most)?
5. Which is more important or effective for teaching: experience or cleverness? Why?
6. Do the teachers in your school have weekly meetings?
7. How many shifts do you teach in a day?
   Hours taught in a week?
8. How many teachers are there in your school?   Males____ Females____
9. What is your education level?
10. How many years have you taught here?
11. How many teaching methods do you know?
    List:
12. Have you had refresher courses?
13. What kind of punishment is used on undisciplined students?

14. What is the impact of school in your community?

15. Proposals:

16. Surveyors' comments:

Students' Interviews:
Students (Group interviews):
Gender and Number interviewed:

1. How old are you?

2. What class (grade) are you studying?

3. What is your father's occupation(s)?

4. How is your teacher's attitude with you? Describe:

5. Are you satisfied with coming to school? Why or why not?

6. Do the classmates and the teachers like you?
Why or why not?

7. What do you do in your leisure time?

8. How many friends do you have?

9. Are your friends coming to school, too?
Why or why not?

10. Are your teachers present on their jobs on time?

11. How many subjects do you study in school?

12. Are you interested in your lessons?

13. Which subjects do you like the most?

14. How many persons are literate in your family? (Who are they?)

15. Do you have books? Show us.

16. Show your pen to us (count).

17. Is there chalk in the class?

18. Is there a blackboard in the class?

19. Do you have problems buying notebooks?

20. Can you afford them?

21. Does the school give you pencils?

22. What do you do with the pencil and pencil sharpener?

23. Are you familiar with models, such as those of the body?

24. What do you want to do when you grow up?

25. Punishment?

26. Proposals:

27. Surveyors' comments:

Community Interviews:

1. What is the name of this area?
2. What is the population? Estimates for the school area ____.
3. What is the economic situation and occupation of people in this area?
4. What is the percentage of literate people in the community?
5. Did the school exist in this area before SO or not?
   How long has it been there?
6. How is the security in the area?
7. Are the people helping/supporting the teachers? Financially or spiritually? Why or why not? Or how?
8. Is transportation available for students?
9. Are you, as a community, satisfied with the way the school is running? Why or why not?
10. What is your opinion regarding improving the school?
11. Surveyors' comments:

CHA Survey
Herat
2001

The interviews in Herat were open-ended discussions that allowed people to talk about psychosocial issues that were important to them. We did not use a series of set questions but had decided on the kinds of issues we wanted to explore in the context of the conversation/interview. The people we talked to were asked if we could speak to them about mental health issues in their communities. Discussions were kept general, and we practiced ways to protect the person being interviewed. We agreed that we would not ask for personal stories but would ask about problems in the community.

Areas to cover if possible included the following:

Explore causes of distress:
Family conflict
Poverty
Prolonged warfare
Political uncertainty
Specific cultural practices
Supernatural phenomena

Negative Coping Mechanisms:
Aggression
Domestic violence
Self-destructive behaviour
  • Drug abuse
  • Suicide
  • Self-harming (burning)

What kinds of health problems do people have?
What do they think are the causes of these health problems?

Look at areas of rapid culture change:
  • Men's issues as they deal with Taliban
  • Women's issues: family/marriage/isolation

Mental health protection (In what ways does Afghan culture support mental health?)
  • Phrase some questions that might get at this level of mental health impact.

Explore emotions and how people display them. Ask person to list both positive and negative emotions. Explore who would show each emotion and how. Who is not allowed to show the emotion. Example: fear (men cannot show fear but women can)

Appendix B

Glossary of Dari Terms

Amir bil Maroof wa Nahi An il-Munkir   The Prevention of Vice and Promotion of Virtue

asaabi   a local term for anxiety

chadari   also called the burqa, a woman's over-garment of fabric attached to a cap and with a mesh through which the woman can see

chador   large shawl worn by women to cover their upper bodies

chowkidar   gatekeeper

hadeez   sayings attributed to the Prophet Mohammed

hijab   a floor-length coat and head scarf

Kafir   unbelievers, non-Muslims

madrasa   religious school

mahram   legal male escort

mujahadeen   often translated as "freedom fighter"; in the Afghanistan context it generally refers to the Afghans who fought against the Soviets

nai   bamboo or reed flute

shalwar kamees   the tunic dress over baggy pants with a tablecloth-sized cotton shawl

soldona   local word for the disease Leishmaniasis, which is a parasite spread by the sandfly

talib   singular of Taliban, literally translates to "a student of Islam"

waqt-e-gul-e-nai   roughly translates to "when bamboo bloom," the Afghan equivalent to "when hell freezes over"

Appendix C

Acronyms

AFSC   American Friends Service Committee, also known as The Quakers
CHA   Coordination of Humanitarian Assistance
CHW   community health worker
CIA   Central Intelligence Agency
IAM   International Assistance Mission
ICRC   International Committee of the Red Cross
IDP   internally displaced person
IOM   International Organization for Migration
LEP   land mine education program
MSF   Médicins Sans Frontières, or Doctors Without Borders
NATO   North Atlantic Treaty Organization
NGO   nongovernmental organization
Novib   Oxfam Novib, the Dutch organization for international development
PID   pelvic inflammatory disease
PTSD   posttraumatic stress disorder
SAVE   Save the Children, U.S
SO   Shuhada Organization
TB   tuberculosis
UNHCR   United Nations High Commissioner for Refugees
UNICEF   United Nations Children's Fund
UTI   urinary track infection
UXOs   unexploded ordnance
V&V   *Amir bil Maroof wa Nahi An il-Munkir*—the Prevention of Vice and Promotion of Virtue
WFP   World Food Programme
WHO   World Health Organization

Notes

[1] Kabul is the capital and largest city of Afghanistan. It is located in Kabul Province.

[2] Kohl, or surma, is a black eyeliner made of lead sulfide. It is used throughout the Middle East and South and Central Asia, usually by women to enhance their eyes but also by young Taliban who were easily recognized from their black turbans and their black lined eyes. For information on the dangers of the use of traditionally made eyeliners see Mohammad Hossein Rahbar, Franklin White, Mubina Agboatwalla, Siroos Hozhabri, and Stephen Luby, Factors associated with elevated blood lead concentrations in children in Karachi, Pakistan. *Bulletin of the World Health Organization.* 2002. 80:769–775. http://www.who.int/bulletin/archives/80(10)769.pdf. For a general description see: http://en.wikipedia.org/wiki/Kohl (cosmetics), (accessed May 20, 2010).

[3] I have changed the names of friends and colleagues in all instances except two. Aziz and Engineer Muslim wanted their names in my book, and because they were an important part of my life and work during this period and after, I have honored their request.

[4] In fact, they remain a major problem around the world and cause as many deaths and injuries as land mines. I recommend a visit to the Web site of the International Campaign to Ban Landmines http://www.icbl.org/intro.php

[5] Nancy Hatch Dupree worked in Afghanistan and Pakistan since the 1960s with her husband, Louis Dupree, and is an authority on Afghan cultural heritage. www.dupreefoundation.org/

[6] A mahram would be the woman's husband, father, brother, son, or any extended family member with whom she could not legally marry (such as her sister's husband).

[7] http://www.iam-afghanistan.org/our-mission-values (accessed July 16, 2010); Médicins Sans Frontières http://www.msf.org (accessed July 16, 2010).

[8] UN data on the extent of the drought and the number of people needing assistance by province: FAO Global Information and Early Warning System on Food and Agriculture World Programme. FAO/WFP Crop and Food Supply Assessment Mission to Afghanistan. 8 June 2001. http://www.fao.org/docrep/004/y1259e/y1259e00.HTM. For information on IDPs, see: http://ocha-gwapps1.unog/ch/rw/rwb.nsf/db900SID/ACOS-64DBQP?Open Document (accessed May 22, 2010).

[9] Citadel of Herat. http://www.archnet.org/library/sites/one-site.jsp?site_id=11348 (accessed February 22, 2009).

[10] Great Mosque of Herat. http://www.archnet.org/library/sites/one-site.jsp?site_id=8210 (accessed February 22, 2009).

[11] "The WHO Health Update for 14 December 2001 indicated that acute respiratory infections, including pneumonia, remained the primary concern for 300,000 people gathered in and around Herat. Tuberculosis is especially a concern in the overcrowded Maslakh camp near Herat. Lobby-

ing had begun for a new IDP camp near Herat so that Maslakh camp can be closed to new arriv-als. The International Organization for Migration (IOM) conducted a full re-registration of all residents of Maslakh camp using scanable bracelets for the heads of family. As of late 2001 Maslakh held an estimated 200,000–300,000 residents." http://www.globalsecurity.org/military/world/afghanistan/herat.htm (accessed February 22, 2009).

References

Barks, Coleman. (1997). *The essential Rumi.* San Francisco: Harper.

Burns, A. August, et al. (1997). *Where women have no doctor: A health guide for women.* Palo Alto: Hesperian Foundation.

CIA. (2010). Central Intelligence Agency. *The World Factbook: Afghanistan.* https://www.cia.gov/library/publications/the-world-factbook/geos/af.html (accessed July 15, 2010).

Doubleday, Veronica. (1990). *Three women of Herat.* Austin: University of Texas Press.

Focusing Institute. (2003). http://www.focusing.org/afghan.asp (accessed February 22, 2009).

Hosseini, Khalid. (2003). *The kite runner.* New York: Riverhead Books.

MSF (Médicin Sans Frontières), Holland. (1999). Mental Health in Herat. Unpublished paper.

Omidian, Patricia. (2001). Afghan aid workers and psychosocial well-being. *The Lancet,* Nov 3.

Omidian, Patricia. (1996). *Aging and family in an Afghan refugee community: Traditions and transitions.* New York: Garland.

Omidian, Patricia. (2007). A community based approach to Focusing: The Islam and Focusing Project of Afghanistan. *The Folio: A Journal for Focusing and Experiential Therapy,* 20(1).

Omidian, Patricia and Nina Joy Lawrence. (2008). Community wellness Focusing: A work in process. *The Folio: A Journal for Focusing and Experiential Therapy,* 21(1):291–303.

Shuhada Organization. (2008). http://www.shuhada.org.af/EngDefault.asp (accessed July 27, 2009).

United Nations. (2009). Human Development Reports. http://hdr.undp.org/en (accessed February 22, 2010).

WHO. (2001). The WHO Health Update for 14 December. http://www.globalsecurity.org/military/world/afghanistan/herat.htm (accessed February 22, 2009).